Memory
and Learning

A Practical Guide for Teachers

Jacqueline Bristow,
Philip Cowley and Bob Daines

Illustrated by Ben Stone

David Fulton Publishers
London

David Fulton Publishers Ltd
Ormond House, 26–27 Boswell Street, London WC1N 3JD

First published in Great Britain by David Fulton Publishers 1999

Note: The rights of Jacqueline Bristow, Philip Cowley and Bob Daines
to be identified as the authors of this work has been asserted by them
in accordance with the Copyright, Designs and Patents Act 1988.

Copyright © Jacqueline Bristow, Philip Cowley and Bob Daines 1999

British Library Cataloguing in Publication Data
A catalogue record for this book is available from the British Library

ISBN 1–85346–594–1

Typeset by FSH Print & Production Ltd
Printed in Great Britain by Bell and Bain Ltd, Glasgow

Contents

Notes on the authors, illustrator and contributors   v

Introduction   ix

1   Human memory   1
Learning physical skills   22
Visual shorthand   24
Differentiation and keywording   28
Keywords and icons   30
Memory and Information Communication Technology   33

2   Memory and language   35
Facilitating memory for language – a strategic approach   49
Reading comprehension and keywording   54
Descriptive writing   55
Essay writing   59
Note-taking   60

3   Memory and education   62
Curriculum subjects and memory   65
Key learning goals at the early stages – Overview   68
Reading – Overview   69
Letters and letter sounds – a mnemonic approach to
    teaching and learning   72
Practical ways of supporting verbal working memory
    in literacy   73
Singing with Jessica   77
Spelling – Overview   78
Mathematics – Overview   80
Remembering basic numbers   82

4   Meta-memory and personal organisation   84
Supporting children with memory difficulties in
    the primary classroom   88
Mastering the school day   92
Remembering appointments, arrangements and deadlines   94
Memory and test and exam revision   95

References   99

Index   101

Notes on the authors, illustrator and contributors

Jacqueline is an Educational Psychologist for Brighton and Hove Council. Her specialism is work with hearing-impaired and deaf children. She has been looking at memory processes in hearing-impaired pupils with colleagues in other professions over a number of years and has been involved in running workshops for teachers on the links between memory and learning.

Jacqueline Bristow

Philip is an Educational Psychologist for Brighton and Hove Council with an interest in communication disorders. He has a long-standing commitment to exploring the working memory processes and movement memory in children's learning and has contributed to many courses and workshops for teachers.

Philip Cowley

Bob is an Educational Psychologist for Brighton and Hove Council. His core professional interest has been in the links between cognitive psychology and children's development and learning. His specialist field is speech and language impairment. Recent publications include the following co-authored books: *Spotlight on Speech and Language Impairment* (NASEN), *Dyspraxia* (Fulton) and the manual for the *Penguin Plays for Reading* (Ginn).

Bob Daines

Ben has been illustrating since he was born. Taught by his mother – another highly respected artist – he has spent most of his career creating graphic images for bands on T-shirts, CDs and record covers, with the occasional dabbling in the advertising industry.

Ben Stone

About the contributors:

Jenny Barrett is a Senior Speech and Language Therapist for the South Downs NHS Trust.

Angela Belliveau is a Speech and Language Therapist for the South Downs NHS Trust.

Pam Fleming is a specialist teacher for speech- and language-impaired children, currently seconded as an assistant educational psychologist.

Carol Hodgson is a primary Special Educational Needs Coordinator.

Jenny Jones is a primary Special Educational Needs Coordinator.

Louise Kelly is a Speech and Language Therapist for the South Downs NHS Trust.

Karen Sandford is a specialist teacher for speech- and language-impaired children.

Christina Zergaeng is an Educational Psychologist for East Sussex and The Children's Head Injury Service, South Downs NHS Trust.

Acknowledgements

This book has come out of joint working with many colleagues. Some of these we have been able to refer to in the book.

We owe Lalagé Tutt a considerable debt for her work in putting the text of the book together and in being able to keep us 'on task'.

Thanks to Lyn Wendon for permission to use the Letterland illustration.

Footfalls echo in the memory

Down the passage, which we did not take

Towards the door we never opened

Into the rose-garden. My words echo

Thus, in your mind.

                    But to what purpose

Disturbing the dust on a bowl of rose-leaves

I do not know.

               Other echoes

Inhabit the garden. Shall we follow?

T. S. Eliot *Four Quartets*
Burnt Norton 1 lines 11-20
Reproduced by permission of Faber & Faber Ltd

Introduction

The purpose of this book is to give detailed practical suggestions to teachers so that their pupils remember more effectively what they have been taught. In order to achieve this, a number of other aims have to be realised:

1. We have to establish a contemporary understanding of human memory and show how a research-based model of the structure of memory comes alive in the everyday remembering and forgetting of both ourselves and our pupils.
2. We need also to address attitudes and assumptions about memory and learning that are prevalent within current educational practice.
3. We need to show, at every age and stage, how we can help pupils to become more aware of their own memory and take more active responsibility for their own remembering by the use of appropriate strategies.

The 'authors' of this book are numerous and various, as it springs from a long history of cooperation in joint projects, in-service training and Individual Educational Plans. Some of the Practice Papers have been contributed by named individuals. As educational psychologists, we have been particularly impressed by the wealth of teacher strategies that derive from the careful cognitive assessment of children with learning difficulties. Theory and assessment can generate possible teaching approaches that teachers then develop in a fuller and rounded way. Teachers' own successful practical strategies also benefit from theory as the reason for their effectiveness can be established, leading to both a wider application and a sharper focus. In addition, the theory can lead to better assessment of the children who would most benefit from particular approaches.

All the contributors to the book work with children who find learning difficult. These children have forced us all to confront the challenge to remember that fills the educational process. We owe them a great debt of thanks. The majority of the practical suggestions are vital if these struggling pupils are to learn. It is, however, very clear that all children benefit from many of the methods and at the very least they often provide a vital safety net which is essential in the inclusive classroom. Many of the practical suggestions are already in use but scattered across the teaching profession. In this book we aim to draw them together, set them in a theoretical context, and show how they can be used more effectively and on a wider basis.

There are two fundamental reasons why practical approaches developed for children who experience learning difficulties have a wider application to all children. Firstly, we do not all learn or carry out tasks in the same way, there are considerable individual differences between all of us. We tend to think of memory as one ability, but research quoted later shows that we have many different types of memory and can be strong at one and weak at another. We all have different memory profiles that influence the way we learn and the way we approach activities. The blanket idea of intelligence and the use of IQs have also helped obscure this fact. Secondly, the different subjects make different demands on our memory. We need to be aware of what these are and how this relates to the individual differences in our students.

The book is divided into four chapters. Each chapter consists of one or more overview sections and Practice Papers. The Practice Papers each take a specific focus.

Chapter 1

Human memory

In our view, the best way to understand the nature of our memory is to reflect on the characteristics of our own remembering and forgetting. There will be large differences between us. Many of these are due to our individual biology. Firstly, there is a sex difference in that males have a bias towards visual memory, particularly spatial memory, i.e. remembering position, distance, etc. Females have a bias towards verbal memory. There is substantial research in this area and it is the most widely accepted constitutional brain-sex difference (Maccoby and Jacklin 1974). This does not mean that all males are better than all females visually or that all females are better than all males verbally. This is because all biological features vary across individuals. We all vary in height but on average males are taller; some females are, however, taller than some males. We should think of visual and verbal memory in the same way. Secondly, as we have just pointed out, we all vary individually. Each of our characteristics vary. In the case of memory this quickly becomes complex, as we do not have just one memory but a number of different memories. We have at least five basic memories and a wide range of secondary memories. Research has long shown that just because you are good at one sort of memory it does not mean that you are good at another. You may be good at remembering stories but poor at remembering pictures (Stevenson *et al.* 1975).

Differences between us also reflect the memory strategies we have developed in order to cope with information. Some of us will also have been taught memory strategies. We now come to our first practical principle. We only tend to use strategies that we feel comfortable with and that work for us. It is a mistake to pick one strategy and teach it to all pupils in a given situation. Some will be able to make it work for them while others won't. This difference in 'comfort' is really about how the strategy in question relates to our underlying memory strengths and weaknesses. In the classroom, the best general approach is to present information in such a way that the widest possible range of memories can be used. From a teaching point of view this is called a multimedia approach. From an individual perspective we call it a multi-memory approach. In special education this is often, inappropriately, referred to as a multisensory approach.

We hope our introduction will make you happier about completing the questionnaire below. You can expect to have difficulties remembering in at least some areas of your life. Our culture overwhelms us with information, and places considerable demands on our memory. There are very few of us who never resort to external memories. You do this as soon as you write anything down for your own reference or as soon as you ask to be reminded about something. Our workplaces are full of written information and we expect pupils to make notes. Read through the following examples of memory lapses and put an 's' for sometimes, an 'o' for often or an 'n' for never, alongside each statement. Later, when we present the basic model of memory, you should be able to see where your own strengths and weaknesses lie.

1. Not remembering when someone says, 'do you remember when we went to X'.
2. Not recognising a place that you have been to before.
3. Being disappointed in how well you play a physical game.
4. Forgetting phone or pin numbers.
5. Losing the thread of the story line, e.g. getting lost in a complex detective story.
6. Searching for a word that is on the 'tip of your tongue'.
7. Forgetting details about your experiences the day before.
8. Driving on the wrong side of the road during, or after, a foreign holiday.
9. Failing to remember an appointment that you were not very keen on.
10. Forgetting to pass on a message, post a letter, or buy something.
11. Forgetting to pay a bill.
12. Getting angry and then forgetting to do something.
13. Getting somebody else to remember something for you.
14. Leaving behind a jumper, coat, hat or umbrella.
15. Returning to check that you have turned off the gas or locked the door.
16. Forgetting some information that you have been told.
17. Accidentally stalling the engine when driving.
18. Telling someone a piece of gossip that you have told them already.
19. Losing your way in a town that you have only been to a few times.
20. Giving directions by turnings but forgetting the names of streets.
21. Not remembering where you left your keys.
22. Forgetting to tell your partner that someone rang.
23. Forgetting the names of your friend's children.
24. Remembering that the hour should change – but forwards or backwards?
25. Forgetting the capital cities of countries.
26. Forgetting how to wire a three-pin plug.

27. Forgetting how to set up the pieces in a game.
28. Forgetting how to toss a pancake.
29. Forgetting how to fold an Ordnance Survey map.
30. Forgetting your way out of a large building.
31. Forgetting someone's birthday.
32. Remembering the answers after you have done the exam.
33. Continuously checking that the doors are locked before going on holiday.
34. Forgetting to cancel the papers before a weekend away.

Each of the above statements emphasises one or more characteristics of our memory. Below we have grouped them together so that they illustrate the basic model of memory. We need, however, to make an initial distinction between recognition and recall (Hintzman *et al.* 1998). We are most aware of our memory when we make an effort to remember. We are then committing all our attention to trying to recall something, i.e. a name, a fact, how to spell a word, where we have seen somebody before or what we were doing last Tuesday lunch time. This process is called recall and involves bringing a memory to consciousness at our own request. The primary process of memory is, however, recognition. We recognise something as familiar. When skilled readers read they recognise all the words; they are familiar, they have seen them before and have learnt (remembered) the spoken word that they symbolise. It is our recognition of the things around us and of the situations and people we meet that largely gets us through the day. The familiar is the basic framework of our life. We often take these memories for granted and fail to acknowledge that we once had to learn them. This is a common occurrence in teaching. It is easy to confuse a pupil's reasoning or intelligence with their memory. This happens when we think that the pupil has failed to see the connection between ideas when in fact they have missed one or more memories: bits of learning. As teachers, we need to be fully aware of what it is that we know about a subject before we can teach it. The hidden knowledge in situations, particularly teaching situations, is called implicit knowledge. We often describe others as intelligent, meaning good at reasoning, when in fact it is their implicit knowledge that has impressed us. The teachers who are good at teaching the weaker pupils are those who bring out, make explicit, the implicit knowledge required. A pupil can easily form a self-image as someone who is unintelligent when in fact they simply lack learning, i.e. key memories. For reasons we will examine later, the individuals who stand out at school are those with the best verbal memories.

The first area of human memory that we are going to look at is *declarative memory*. This name is used because the memories can be declared, i.e. talked about, even though both the memories in this area contain much that cannot easily be accessed by language. The two key memories involved are *episodic memory* and *semantic memory*. *Episodic memory* is your record of the episodes that have happened to you. What you experienced when you went to the charity shop last Saturday is stored in a connected way. What you said, who you met, what you bought, an object that you reacted to with disgust because it had not been cleaned, the smell of the freshly painted door and the sound of the rain shower starting up as you sorted through the ties, are all stored in a connected way in your episodic memory. They will also be stored separately and in other ways in different memories. Like all memories, episodic memories begin fresh and detailed and then fade, unless there is a reason for remembering them. We remember most vividly the episodes that have just happened to us; I can remember a lot that happened half an hour ago, when I made myself a cup of tea in the kitchen. Nearly all of it trivial and of no importance. We can talk in surprising detail of recent events in our lives. After a few weeks we might remember nothing about our visit to the charity shop. If, however, something of importance, or something that we reacted to strongly, occurred, then we might well remember the visit in much more detail. Our reaction of disgust may have been so strong that it itself becomes a strong memory, or we may have purchased a favourite tie there. If just one memory from the episode becomes important then we will remember rather than forget some of the other details.

It is easy to see the value of this in our lives. Significant memories or experiences need to be linked to those situations in which they occurred so that if the situations recur we will recognise the possibilities inherent in them and explore them purposefully. The more significant a key experience is for us, the more likely we are to remember the detail of the episode and of other episodes occurring around that time. We can all think of many examples of this point. In the questionnaire, the statements that point to this memory are:

1. Not remembering when someone says, 'do you remember when we went to X'.
2. Not recognising a place that you have been to before.
7. Forgetting details about your experiences the day before.
19. Telling someone a piece of gossip that you have told them already.
23. Forgetting to tell your partner that someone rang.

Research shows that information, even that given in lectures to undergraduates, is initially most strongly linked to the teaching situation rather than to a network of meanings (*semantic memory*) (Conway *et al.* 1997). Facts that are linked together by meanings can also often be linked in episodes by recreating their historical or geographical context. This is done by acting out or dramatising. In any area of knowledge that is just beginning to be mastered, teaching through episodes is a good place to begin. This is why it is a strategy commonly found in the teaching of young children. Acting out a Roman meal or a Victorian classroom is not just a matter of keeping children interested, it also lays the foundations of some important knowledge (memories/ learning). Talk teaching can sometimes overwhelm pupils and students with verbal information that is quickly lost to verbal memory (this is discussed later) and that they cannot place in their semantic memory because they don't know enough about the subject. It is not then learnt but is lost or forgotten. The availability of episodic memory can prevent this happening. For the same reasons, teachers take pupils on trips and visits, and museums attempt to bring their objects to life. Episodic memory can be strangely powerful; just standing by the power station

while listening to a lecture on electricity generation can make it much more likely that you will remember the content of the lecture. It is not every day you stand next to a power station.

This is in itself a core memory around which other details, even the lecture content, can hang. The same familiar classroom, sitting in the same seat and using the same book and pen all deprive episodic memory of opportunities. Episodic memory could be used more widely with older and more knowledgeable pupils. It is, however, right that it falls into the background as it is gradually replaced by semantic memory as the main vehicle for storing subject knowledge; semantic memory can be built up quickly using talk teaching. Episodic memory contains redundant experiences and features and is time consuming. You might well remember the approximate length of a Roman sword but you also remember that you felt sick after eating the egg sandwiches. As we have seen, episodic memory is vital for new learning however, and should figure particularly prominently in the teaching of young children.

As our experience is increasingly mapped in language, episodic memory can contain details of episodes that other people have experienced. Clearly this is second hand and the sensory content is not as rich and can only be imagined. However, a vast vista of episodes is opened up; we know these as stories. Through stories, episodic memory is greatly expanded and the possibilities of a larger base for semantic memory thereby also enlarged. This interaction between story and meaning is fundamental to knowledge acquisition, particularly in the primary years, and acts as the bedrock for subject divisions. Story never fully replaces experience. We can learn from the account of a physics experiment but to witness or, better still, carry out the experiment is more memorable (more effective for learning).

As previously discussed, we all vary in the quality of our episodic memory. Some individuals have a very good overall memory for their experiences while in others it is poor. For those good at it, it can be used as a source of *mnemonics*. These are very important and we will attempt an account of them before continuing; a mnemonic is simply something that helps you remember something else. It only works because it is easier to remember than the target memory and is reliably linked to it. Turning the first letters of your shopping list into an anagram is not much help if you forget the anagram. Similarly, tying a knot in your handkerchief is no good if you then forget what it was supposed to remind you of. The rules of choosing a mnemonic are therefore that it should be easy to remember and should have a reliable link to the target memory. The courses that you see advertised claiming that you can improve your memory simply teach mnemonic systems of one kind or another. Mnemonics have to be chosen in relation to your individual strengths and weaknesses. There are some necessary but difficult-to-remember aspects of school learning that routinely benefit from some standard mnemonics. These will be referred to later in the book. Every type of memory can be used as a source of mnemonics for recalling details located in other memories. Episodic memory can be used to recall things by association within a shared situation; if there is no shared situation then the association will simply be in your verbal memory. Again, we discuss this later.

How is episodic memory used as a source of mnemonics? The fundamental process is using a real or recalled situation in order to remember a detail. Going into the shed might help you remember where you put the new door hinge. Imagining going into the shed could have the same effect. Recalling the situations in which you learnt something can help you remember the details. Research shows that even undergraduates initially depend on this memory, as they often report that they remember things by recalling where they learnt them, which lecture for example. As they progress through their course, the research shows that they are using semantic memory more. They report that they simply 'know things' (Conway *et al.* 1997). Early learning of new topics is enhanced if the situation in which they are taught is memorable in a wide range of unrelated ways. One of the easiest ways of doing this in the classroom is to engage pupils' emotional responses. Of the emotions, surprise is probably the most easily included; even the maths teacher untypically wearing a floral pink shirt might get quadratic equations off to a better start!

It is interesting to reflect that the Victorians made effective use of fear within the classroom experience as an aid to learning. Opportunities within new learning to trigger empathy with the subject content should be looked for. For this purpose, any of the basic emotions could be used: anger, surprise, sadness, happiness, disgust or fear. Being clear when something is taught is also helpful. Teachers often help pupils remember by saying things like 'we covered it at the end of last term'. They could usefully add to this by giving more situational detail, e.g. 'we studied that on the day of the last fire drill'.

A popular trick mnemonic uses a combination of episodic and visual–semantic memory. This is described at the end of the section on visual memory.

The other declarative memory is *semantic memory*. This contains the main human store of knowledge and is concerned entirely with meaning. It is often popularly thought to be a language memory but this is not the case; the contents of semantic memory are not connected by syntax or grammar. In other words, information is not stored in phrases or sentences; much of the contents of semantic memory can, however, be quickly expressed in phrases and sentences. Individual words do, however, play a central, although by no means exclusive, part: it is the meaning of the words that counts. Words are linked together by their meanings but they are also linked to other sensory information, particularly visual. The memory has sections that deal with each of the senses but it is primarily extremely rich with images and pictures. Semantic memory has largely been excluded from research because it is such a complex and widespread memory (Baddeley 1997). It seems to be fundamentally made up of general points derived from our experience or passed on to us by others, usually through language (ibid.). It works like a map of reality and its structure is best captured through diagrams linking words, rather than through detailed verbal accounts. The best sense that we have of this is the way we recognise that there is a clear difference between the meaning of an object, i.e. what it is connected to, and its name.

The questions in our questionnaire that point to this memory are:

5. Losing the thread of a story line, e.g. getting lost in a complex detective story.

25. Remembering that the hour should change – but forwards or backwards?

Figure 1.1 effectively shows the main types of connection in semantic memory.

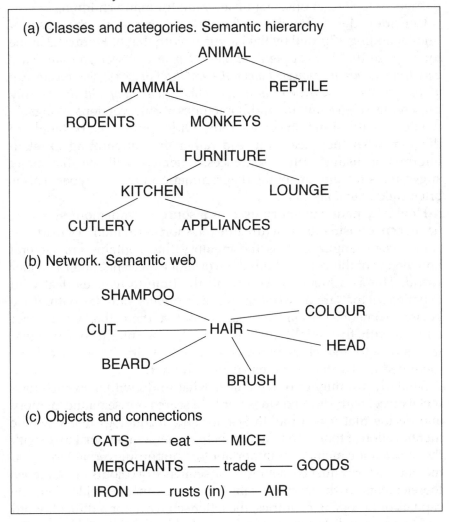

Figure 1.1 The main types of connection in semantic memory

Information in computer software is now stored on an objects and connections basis. A computer encyclopaedia, although presenting printed sentences to the user, actually now stores the information in a similar way to us, i.e. by word linking. In education, it is the semantic memory that we are primarily trying to develop. In our culture we tend to assume that the main way to develop meaning is through language, and we ignore the fact that there are other routes. This is particularly true at secondary level. The use of multimedia approaches is undoubtedly the most effective way of teaching and learning, but their use is severely limited by their cost. The semantic memory can, however, be accessed directly in any classroom by using diagrams that link together keywords (concepts). Any of the three types of diagram in Figure 1.2 can be used. Teachers could present their information both as traditional text (sentences) and diagrammatically. As we will consider later, accessing the semantic memory through the verbal memory, i.e. through language, can be highly inefficient. There is considerable experience within teaching that many children do not have the language ability, or have good enough verbal memories, to process the constant complex language through which they are taught. Verbal ability and verbal 'load' act as barriers to the target of semantic learning for many children.

Consider the following example and compare the ease of understanding afforded by the language with that of Figure 1.2 at the top of page 10. '*A candle placed at the bottom of a jar soon goes out, but if a partition is carefully lowered down the middle of the jar so that the top half of the jar has a partition in it the candle will stay alight.*' Simply presenting diagrammatic and sometimes iconic versions alongside would ease the situation considerably. Older pupils can be taught to diagram what they hear and read rather than attempting to retain information using written sentences. Later we will see that many suggested strategies are of the diagrammatic and iconic types. This is often called *mind mapping*.

How is semantic memory used as a source of mnemonics? As we have seen, utilising its structure lifts the short-term memory load that comes from language. It is the memory that contains our general knowledge of the world – both the world of experience and the wider world. This is a memory we use all the time to help us deal with experiences that are new or that we are not very familiar with. If we go into someone's room and see an object there that we are not familiar with, they might say 'it is a chair', or we might conclude that it belongs to the class of objects called chairs. When we have identified it as a chair we then try and sit on it.

Similarly, we might not remember what to do with a six-inch long metal object with serrated sides until we search our semantic memory and decide that it is a file. In Science and Technology, the semantic identification of tools and materials helps us remember what to do with them. Semantic memory is important for supporting verbal long-term memory, list or sequence memory. The sequence of colours in a rainbow, the elements in the periodic table, the notes in the treble cleft, the capitals of European countries, the letter sequence for a difficult word and many other lists can often only be reliably remembered by using a semantic mnemonic. The most common way is to take the initial letter sound of each of the words in the list and, keeping the order, use them as the first sounds of new words that together create a memorable sentence picture. An example would be the list of planets in order of their distance from the sun. The initial letters are M(Mercury), V(Venus), E(Earth), M(Mars), J(Jupiter), S(Saturn), U(Uranus), N(Neptune), P(Pluto). A memorable picture sentence could be 'My Very Enormous Monster Just Swallowed Up Nasty Peter'. With spellings, each letter, again in the same order, is used as the first sound of a word. The words together create a sentence meaning picture. A well-known target for this kind of attention is the word 'because', e.g. *Big Elephants Can Always Upset Small Earwigs*.

This is a rich area for strategies and these are explored more fully later in the book. They are extremely easy to devise. Most subjects

have many examples of sequences where the items don't link together in a way that retains their critical order. In all cases these should be taught with a mnemonic of the semantic type, but they very rarely are. Teachers often argue that these mnemonics give the pupils more to remember. This is an entirely mistaken assumption. A good semantic mnemonic, with strong unusual meaning of a picturable kind, will be remembered far more easily than the list of planets in the correct order. Degree-level Chemistry students at Oxbridge continue to access the periodic table by using such mnemonics.

We will now turn our attention to *procedural memory*. This is almost the opposite of declarative, episodic and semantic memory, in that the memory cannot be accessed by language. This does not mean that there is no connection between procedural memory and language; our conscious thinking in verbal memory, drawing on other memories, can be used to notice or comment on what the procedural memory is getting us to do. The procedural memory is a 'doing' memory and is fundamental to our animal nature and to our bodies. It is probably best thought of as a body memory. One of the most famous illustrations of the separateness of this memory is the anecdote about the doctor who put a pin in his hand to shake the hand of a brain-damaged patient. This patient had lost his episodic memory, so his experiences were lost to his awareness. The next day the patient refused to shake the doctor's hand although he couldn't say why, and had no memory of the previous day's incident.

We are often challenged by others, and sometimes challenge ourselves, as to why we do things or why we do them in a particular way. These questions only have access to our verbal memory, and through this, our semantic and episodic memory. The correct answer to these questions is usually 'I don't know'. Sometimes we say, 'I have forgotten'. This is not a correct observation. Strictly speaking we should say, 'I don't have access to that memory'. We always feel, however, that we *should* know and that we should be able to justify ourselves. It may be that our conscious memories have been noticing and can offer an attempted explanation; we usually try to come up with reasons. In many cases these will be entirely fictitious although plausible. There is a value in asking, 'Why did you do that?' It is a question used to a lot of children. It serves to engage the conscious mind in noticing our actions and behaviour. Such 'noticing' can lead us to make deliberate changes that through repetition, i.e. practice; become procedural, what we sometimes call automatic. Suggesting that someone holds their pen in a different way, holds their tennis racket further up the handle or stops rolling their rubber off the desk are examples of this process. Our procedural memory therefore includes all our adaptations, preferences, habits and conditioning. It also includes the major part of all our practical skills. An important part of this memory is our body's knowledge of how to physically move in different situations; these memories accumulate over life. Examples include learning how to hold a cup, ride a bike, plane a piece of timber, do handwriting, drive a car and play sports. The key to good remembering in procedural memory is repetition and practice, although conscious learning can be helpful. It is more effective to demonstrate and manipulate pupils through movements than it is to

Figure 1.2

talk about what to do. There is currently far too much talk about practical skills and not enough opportunities to demonstrate and practise. Our culture seriously overestimates what can be achieved through language. Do we want pupils who can comment verbally on a practical skill or who can actually do it? As we have seen, there is a very weak connection between talk of what we do and what we actually do. I may be able to write a very good essay on how to make a soufflé and yet be very poor at actually making one. Good verbal and semantic memories have a limited usefulness in the practical world.

The questions on the questionnaire that point towards procedural memory are:

3. Being disappointed in how well you play a physical game.
8. Driving on the wrong side of the road during, or after, a foreign holiday.
15. Leaving behind a jumper, coat, hat or umbrella.
16. Returning to check that you have turned off the gas or locked the door.

This is a particularly good example of the trouble that your conscious (talkable) memories can cause your procedural memory. When you think 'did I turn off the gas' you are asking your episodic memory. Your turning off the gas would actually occur at a routine level and may well go unnoticed by episodic memory. You then conclude, from your episodic memory, that you can't remember and go back and check. If, as you turned off the gas, a beetle surprised you by crawling over a nearby pan, you might remember because the incident would be more strongly registered in your episodic memory.

18. Accidentally stalling the engine when driving.
22. Not remembering where you left your keys.
27. Forgetting how to wire a three-pin plug.
29. Forgetting how to toss a pancake.
30. Forgetting how to fold an Ordnance Survey map.

One of the authors can fold these maps by remembering the movement sequence while another more poorly coordinated author has to use his visual memory to look at the pattern of creases.

How is procedural memory a source of mnemonics? The most productive way is through movement patterns. There is a considerable amount of clinical evidence from teaching language-impaired children that it is easier to remember a movement sign for an object or event than it is a spoken word. The physical sign for the objects that we use as, and call, 'chairs' is easier to remember than the word 'chair'. This fact is used in teaching language-impaired children. They are taught the sign at the same time as they are taught the spoken word. The sign helps them remember the spoken word and they can often be seen signing to themselves as a means of remembering. These movements or gestures are then internalised. Joint research involving one of the authors a number of years ago showed that self-signing could help all children learn to read words that are hard to remember despite their frequency, e.g. words such as 'there', 'when', 'out' and 'or' (Ripley and Daines 1990). Invented or established sign systems can be used in this highly selected way to focus on key spoken and written words. The signs are not learned for communication but as a mnemonic. Already, in some educational practice, signs are used to help children remember number words. Those individuals with good coordination, part of which involves a good movement memory, can often use movements to remember for example telephone, pin or bus numbers. Simply trace the numbers, in sequence, in the air with whole arm movements. Not strictly a mnemonic, but nevertheless a powerful memory strategy, is to incorporate new things that you need to remember to do into an existing routine, rather than relying on verbal memory. Instead of saying to yourself 'I must remember to open the airing cupboard door in the morning', practise your early morning routine and add in, at a sensible point, opening the airing cupboard door. This is a case of changing a routine or procedure and requires practice rather than a note in your verbal memory. It is another case of the inappropriate use of a conscious memory. Similarly, behaviour in pupils is better changed by practice and taking them through routines than by verbal requests. If you want them to put their chairs firmly under their tables before they go out of the classroom then practise it. The debate between education and training is resolved by considering the nature of the learning that is required. Procedural learning is a matter for training as long as evaluation and decisions are not involved.

The next memory to consider is *visual/spatial memory*. The word 'visual' points us towards the wealth of images we recognise and recall, while the word 'spatial' indicates the aspect that is to do with the relative position of points. This is a complex area of perception but it is essentially about remembering where something is in relation to what is around it. In a teaching context you could show a child a picture of a farmyard scene. After taking it away you might ask them what they can remember. Let us say the reply is 'pig', 'tractor', 'pond', 'gate', and 'ducks'. The child is using their memory for the images. If you then asked 'Where was the tractor?' the child might then say 'Next to the pond'. They would now be using spatial information.

In this example we are using language to establish visual and spatial knowledge. This happens commonly in schools. It occurs when we give instructions such as 'The pencils are by the rubbers'. Instructions like this often fail because in practice we can see the situation in our visual memory and know where they are. We assume that our language carries all the information the child needs but in fact it carries very little. All the information in language is of a general nature and we have to speak elaborately in order to talk about particular places and objects. In situations like this, it is better not to give verbal directions but to ask a child who knows where the rubbers are to show the child who does not. It is also a serious mistake to draw conclusions about a child's visual memory from what they say. A more appropriate test would be to ask them to choose the correct images of the farm scene from a larger set of images and then arrange them in the correct positions on a blank piece of card. This is yet another·example of how we overrate our conscious talkable memories.

Our visual memory is not made up of static pictures but changes in the same way that a camera scans a scene or follows as the scene unfolds.

It is important with visual/spatial memory to make a distinction between short-term and long-term memory. Over the last two decades, the critical role of short-term memory in our everyday functioning has been fully explored, particularly by Alan Baddeley and colleagues (Baddeley 1997). Short-term memory, now referred to as *working memory*, is made up of three components: a visual sketchpad, a speech–sound/verbal memory and a central executive that keeps the two working closely together. The speech–sound memory is referred to in the research literature as the *phonological working memory*; traditionally it is referred to as the auditory/verbal memory. In this book we will term it the *verbal working memory* and will discuss it in the next section.

The sketchpad is used for images and visual details that we have just seen, and for those that we are currently imagining. It is therefore described as a working memory, in that it works on what comes in visually and on the visual material that we already have in our heads. If you are asked which cuddly toy you have just put in the box, you use the sketchpad as you do if you are asked to imagine a lion with two heads. Visual long-term memory is complex and diverse, as episodic, semantic, and procedural memory all contain visual images and visual details. In practice it is better to think of visual long-term memory in terms of the visual aspects of these three, rather than as a separate memory. The sketchpad is, however, quite distinct. The most fundamental educational principle to extract from this picture of short-term memory is that visual and verbal information are always combined, both when we take in information and when we think about subjects, ideas and topics. Our episodic and semantic memories are themselves complex structures containing combinations of the visual and the verbal. It is always best to present new learning using both words and objects, images and diagrams. Listening benefits from looking, and vice versa. To simply talk on any topic is to render individuals dependent on their existing imagery. At the same time as we 'tell', we should 'illustrate', 'show' and 'demonstrate'.

The questions that relate to visual/spatial memory are:

2. Not recognising a place that you have been to before.

20. Losing your way in a town that you have only been to a few times.

21. Giving directions by turnings but forgetting the names of streets.

31. Forgetting your way out of a large building.

How is the visual/spatial memory a source of mnemonics? This memory is the most extensively used for memory aiding and could be used to an even greater extent than it is. It is primarily used for external memories. We don't remember all the information that we need, and rely on various small visible marks arranged on paper in a certain way to code our speech. When we look at these marks we can construct the spoken language that they represent and therefore access much of our memory. You will recognise this as writing and reading, which we have used for thousands of years. The use of drawn patterns (including writing), images and diagrams to make a permanent record on materials such as paper is what we know as books. Computers ape this form of representation in a more flexible and fluid way. An important educational issue is what information do we want pupils to know directly and what information do we want them to know how to access when they need it. Unless it is needed in our daily life then generally detailed information is very easily forgotten. We are often impressed when individuals display knowledge of details such as naming all the capital cities or English football grounds, but this information is better left to external memories such as books and databases. It is always worthwhile, however, to attempt to build semantic memory. This literally maps meaningful connections and allows us to travel to the points where we then start to look for the detail we require.

Before writing, recording was done using little quickly drawn pictures or icons. These acted as a really good memory aid for the person that devised them but others found them hard to interpret. Children with verbal memory and language problems often have serious written language difficulties as well. They can make very good use of quick iconic drawing to help them remember. The icons are generally used to represent instructions or key words and concepts. Increasingly, special needs departments in secondary schools are providing icons for the key words that they have already picked out for their students. Self-generated icons are sometimes preferable. Pupils need to be taught how to do this. Icons are not meant for other people and others are not meant to know what the drawings represent. For the individual pupil who has drawn them, they can be a valuable support in handling some of the information that they are exposed to in school. This area is covered in more detail in the Practice Papers that follow. All pupils should be taught how to do icons and should feel able to use them should they feel a need to when taking notes and instructions. Similarly, linking key words together in diagrams, which uses spatial memory, sometimes called mind mapping, should be more widely encouraged.

There are two common pure mnemonics that use visual memory. Both begin with the need to remember a random list of items. They are therefore mnemonics designed to support verbal memory. The list could be a shopping list or a list of items that you need to take on

holiday. Let us say the list is shaving cream, spare contact lenses, film for the camera, socks, flannel, detective novel and foreign currency. The first mnemonic involves imagining a very familiar room. You imagine yourself going into the room and placing each of the items that you need to remember in a different location as you walk round the room. For example, as you enter the room you put the shaving cream on the chair by the door and then the spare contact lenses by the plug socket for the lamp and so on. When you want to remember the items you imagine the room and then careful walk round it. This mnemonic is good for keeping the sequence of items. A more powerful mnemonic that is less reliable on sequence but does retain the items, involves constructing an imaginary episode, therefore combining episodic and visual memory. Imagine yourself taking a blurred picture (you realise that you haven't got your contact lenses in) of a detective wiping shaving cream off his face with a flannel while wearing only his socks and arguing with a foreigner who won't accept his currency.

The technique of constructing an imaginary eposide is such a powerful mnemonic that the example leaves the impression that we thought of the episode before the list of items. This is not the case. Memory feats for random detail often use this mnemonic and far more can be remembered than even the best verbal memory can achieve, especially if the episode is turned into a story sequence. This mnemonic is so powerful that it has historical and anthropological importance. The oral tradition was, and where it remains is, not dependent on verbal memory. It uses story, episodic memory, and this mnemonic in particular where the actual words need to be remembered. It is still the best mnemonic to use for learning poetry today. Ted Hughes discusses and illustrates this in his book *By Heart: 101 Poems to Remember* (Hughes 1997). He quotes St Thomas Aquinas: 'Man cannot understand without images'.

The final memory that we will focus on is the *phonological/verbal memory*. The word phonological refers to the sounds of speech and is sometimes called auditory. When we have learned language and are awake this memory is almost constantly switched on and we seem to either talking be to others or to ourselves. It also seems to be providing a running commentary on our experiences and our other memories. Psychologists increasingly think of this memory as coming to dominate what we call consciousness. Because this memory is centre stage it tends to overshadow the other memories. This leads to mistakes and missed opportunities in the education of children and students. We popularly assume we have one memory and that this is it. If we can't put it into words in our heads or talk these words to somebody else then we don't remember, understand or know. We can even do ignorant things like asking a potter how he makes such attractive pots. We would be better asking him to show us how he does it. We discussed this point more fully when considering procedural memory.

By leaving this memory until last we have hopefully shown that there is a lot more to our memory than our conscious verbal thinking. When we share our understanding with others, or ourselves by reflecting – i.e. when we express the contents of our semantic memory, and when we share our experience; i.e. when we express the contents of our episodic memory – we use our verbal memory as a support and intermediary. It helps us organise what we are trying to communicate, not least by providing phrases and sentences. It is therefore easiest to confuse our verbal and semantic memories because they do work very closely together. As we have seen, we can, however, express much of our semantic memory pictorially and diagrammatically.

The phonological/verbal memory is based on our perception and use of the sounds of speech. Like the visual/spatial memory, it is vital to divide it into short-term (working) and long-term memory. Our working memory for speech works very closely with our working memory for what we see, i.e. the sketchpad. We use it when we are listening to what is being said and also when we are thinking in language ourselves. We are therefore using it when we are thinking what to say and what to write. Research shows that children who are poor at this memory are slower to learn the names of things, i.e. to build a vocabulary. They also find it harder to learn to read and spell (Gathercole 1990).

The general effect of being weak in this memory is to forget more easily what is said to you, hence it is the major reason for pupils not following instructions and details. Recent research shows that even comprehending what you are reading is more difficult if you are poor at this memory (Oakhill *et al.* 1997). This is probably because when we read we turn the visual marks into inner speech before searching for the meaning. Talking carries a lot of information quickly and is widely used in teaching. By far the majority of children who are struggling in their learning are weak at this memory and require mnemonics from the other memories. These, and an even larger group with strong biases towards the practical and the visual, could do much better in school if their strengths were included in the teaching and learning process. Being good at this memory consists of being able to remember what has been said, even though few links can be made with either the visual memory or with word meaning. Such information can be helpful and can therefore be remembered in verbal long-term memory. The items in such a memory don't link together, i.e. one item doesn't contain any clues pointing to the next item, and hence this memory is often called a list memory. Below are some areas of learning dependent on it:

- names of every sort
- the spoken counting sequence
- number bonds
- tables
- the sequence of days of the week, months of the year
- the dates that link to historical occasions
- the order of notes in the treble cleft
- the order of elements in the periodic table
- the procedures for number operations
- equations
- different types of rock.

Given these few examples, it is easy to generate many more from all the subject areas of the curriculum. These memories fade quickly without constantly being used and rehearsed. They fade even more quickly for those with a weakness in this memory, as well as requiring much more rehearsal to learn in the first place. Hence some pupils can seem to know things at some points in their schooling and not at others.

Slightly more unexpectedly, pupils weak in this memory also have difficulties with:

- mental arithmetic – this is a 'talking to oneself' procedure (although, as we will see later, there are other ways of doing mental arithmetic);
- writing essays – points that have been thought of but are not currently being written need to be stored in this memory, as does the overall plan for the essay;
- examinations – pupils tend to do much better course work and are let down by their poor memory for detail and the poor organisation of their essays.

From the examples above it is clear that a good verbal memory can allow you to perform well in school and can obscure possible weaknesses in the other memories. The reverse is of course also true. Pupils who can't do exams, who can't write good essays and who can't remember talkable details ('facts') can nevertheless have good understanding – semantic memory – and good practical ability – procedural and visual/spatial memory. In addition, information technology (IT) actively supports the verbal memory and hence the increasingly important issue of IT ability is not predictable from the normal ways of assessing children's learning.

Some teachers muddle semantic memory – understanding – and verbal memory, in such a way that they then fail to recognise the information that needs to be learnt by heart. All the example areas above can only be learnt by drill, i.e. by rehearsal and practice. The most common examples are the days of the week for young children, and tables for older pupils. Before embarking down this route, however, teachers need to be clear that the 'facts' in question do need to be committed to memory and can't just be treated as matters of reference. The questions that relate to this memory are:

4. Forgetting phone or pin numbers.

6. Searching for a word that is on the 'tip of your tongue'.

10. Forgetting to pass on a message, post a letter or buy something.

17. Forgetting some information that you have been told.

24. Forgetting the names of your friend's children.

26. Forgetting the capital cities of countries.

32. Forgetting someone's birthday.

How does verbal memory work as a mnemonic? Given the culture we live in, this memory is usually in need of mnemonics from elsewhere, but for those who have a strength in this area it offers the following possibilities. If you have a good verbal memory you can use a date or time sequence very well. Experiences in the past can be tagged with dates to locate them more accurately, and events during the day or future events can be remembered reliably. You are more likely to remember to do things that are out of routine or that need to happen at a certain time of the day. You can even use number codes to remember things such as items on a shopping list. Verbal memory also gives access to semantic memory. You might not remember some key ideas in a description, story or poem but might be able to remember verbatim the text or spoken script. You will be using verbal memory at this point. Going through the verbatim account will take you to the points needed. Strength in this memory also makes you less dependent on external memories such as databases, address books, notes and telephone books. Very few individuals have a good enough verbal memory to handle the sheer volume of detail needed in modern life.

We now need to consider two other important aspects of memory. The first is the role of emotion. We have already touched on this when considering episodic memory. Within episodic and semantic memory each emotion, such as anger, fear, surprise, happiness, sadness, disgust and embarrassment, has its own bank of memories. Once you remember an incident that made you angry you are more likely to remember other incidents or reasons for anger. Facts or ideas that you learnt in a particular emotional state are more likely to be remembered in that state (Eich 1995). One reason why anxiety (fear) causes forgetting in exams is because it is unlikely to correspond to the state you were in when you learnt the material. The main reason, however, is because fear causes a narrowing of attention 'tunnel memory' and impairs verbal working memory (Idzibowski and Baddeley 1983).

As a general principle, the presence of an emotion, even in a small amount (i.e. being slightly surprised), increases the likelihood of surrounding experiences or information being remembered. In teaching young children, experience has led teachers towards gently tapping into their emotional responses. This is usually done through the intermediary of story characters. At every level of education, an element of surprise can help information to be remembered. As we noted earlier, this is probably the emotion that lends itself most easily to learning. From a personal perspective, emotions give things a personal meaning or value, and form the basis for strong associations. You can therefore remember things by deliberately introducing an emotion. A very strongly felt emotion can, however, disrupt and distort learning. The feeling for this point is probably best captured by an expression such as 'I was so angry that I couldn't think straight'.

Questions in the questionnaire that address this are:

12. Getting angry and then forgetting to do something.

33. Remembering the answers after you have done the exam.

34. Continuously checking that the doors are locked before going on holiday.

A second important aspect of memory to consider is the role of intention. Personal relevance and usefulness is a strong constraint on memory. We are not computers but animals and our memory systems are designed to serve our general wellbeing and survival. We have to have implicit or explicit reasons to remember. Our mental processes, including our memories, are constantly being restructured to meet our current life situation. This change in relevance and the results of restructuring are the main reasons that we forget. External reasons for remembering are largely only effective while the reason continues to be present. Tests and exams are external reasons for remembering.

Once the exam is over, what is remembered will be related to such features as how interested we were in all or part of the content, whether we judge that the information will be useful in the future and whether or not we continue to study the subject or topic. All subjects contribute at least fragments to semantic memory but this varies greatly between individuals. Information learnt solely because of external requirements and remembered for external reasons, such as passing an exam, is going to be largely forgotten, and for the individuals concerned the learning experience will therefore have little educational value. Reassurances that the information will be needed in the future, or will be in the memory when required can be spurious. Having said this, information, skills and ideas that have once been learnt will be easier to relearn. This effect is called *priming*. It also operates where information has been registered but cannot yet be actively remembered. Priming is best viewed as the first stage of learning. The second stage would be recognition and the final stage recall. We learn and remember most at the level of priming, and least at the level of conscious recall. When someone says they have forgotten everything they learnt at school, what they mean is that they can't consciously recollect it. They may be surprised at how much they remember at a priming and recognition level. The intention to remember constitutes a deliberate attempt on the part of the individual to remember. It consists of conscious strategies:

1. Making an effort to attend.
2. Going over the material in one's head. Putting it for rehearsal in verbal working memory or imagining it in sketchpad working memory or, more usually, a complex combination of both.
3. Revisiting the experience or episode (episodic).
4. Going over the thinking (semantic).
5. Practising a routine or physical skill (procedural).
6. The deliberate use of *external memories*. The use of homework diaries, home–school books and note taking in lessons are good examples. Good use of these requires recording in the first place and making the effort to consult these memories later on.

Motivating students to make deliberate efforts to remember is a vital part of schooling. Pupils will still make an assessment, this time more consciously, of the personal relevance of using these strategies. We always need, therefore, to help pupils find implicit and explicit reasons for remembering. Anxiety can be helpful with the intention to remember. If anxiety is associated with what has to be remembered it will keep coming back into your mind. If someone is going to be angry if you don't remember to buy the bread, or if you will get detention if you don't do your homework, then you are more likely to remember because the anxiety leads directly to the thoughts coming back to you. This is particularly true if you tap into the anxiety file itself. If a parent makes a child worried about what they have to do for school, they are opening the correct file and memories will be recalled. Similarly, there is a place for teachers gently raising pupils' anxiety in relation to work they have to do and things they have to remember. We all have very different anxiety thresholds, and some pupils may not register anxiety while others become over-anxious. This variation has to be attended to very carefully by teachers. The anxiety itself also has the effect of switching on the individual's intention to remember. Being responsible to other people involves what is termed social anxiety. Research shows that intentions involving other people, such as appointments and meetings, are less likely to be forgotten than intentions involving inanimate objects, such as remembering to collect a form (Meacham and Kushner 1980).

We are now going to consider some facts from studies of the development of children's memory that have strong implications for schooling.

The first point is that young children are very dependent on their visual memories. The visual memory has a very powerful recognition ability. One study showed that 35 years after graduation from high school, adults recognised photographs of their classmates with 90 per cent accuracy. In comparison, they recognised less than 15 per cent of their names (Bahrick *et al.* 1975). The visual memory is paramount in making the world familiar. A young child's semantic memory, the main target memory throughout education, is very dependent on and responsive to visual images. Language does not yet have as much richness of meaning as it does for the ten-year-old pupil and if spoken to at length without illustrations then little may be remembered. A child with a good verbal memory may be able to repeat much of what has been said but questioning can show that little has been understood. By contrast, four-year-olds remember lengthy series of pictures with near perfect accuracy (Brown and Campion 1972). Teachers have again adapted to their experience of teaching young children and they make heavy use of pictures and objects. From the age of six until eleven, the ability to learn directly through language develops; a young child will prefer a visual strategy where an older child will use a verbal one. When shown a tray of objects to remember by name, a ten-year-old is likely to recite the names of the objects, possibly also grouping them semantically (according to the area of life they come from, for example), while a six-year-old is more likely to attempt to picture the objects in the arrangement in which they were presented and then name them from the picture in their head. Secondary-age pupils who continue to have difficulties with language will still be dependent on visualisation.

The second key point from development studies is that young children are not able to use deliberate memory strategies. Young children do not rehearse very effectively (verbal memory), do not group material according to semantic similarity, i.e. put all the animals together and all the clothes, household tools, toys etc., and suggest few solutions for real-world memory problems, (Kail 1979) e.g. ways of trying to remember how you got your favourite cuddly toy. When asked to remember a telephone number or an item from one of the maths tables, only about 10 per cent of five-year-olds will rehearse in their verbal memory. The percentage rises to 60 per cent for seven-year-olds and 85 per cent for ten-year-olds (Flavell *et al.* 1966). This research dates back to the Sixties and Seventies but recent research (1993 and 1994) confirms that children deliberately rehearse at about seven. We give these references in Chapter 1. When shown, young children can use rehearsal very effectively (Flavell *et al.* 1966). This suggests that children should be deliberately taught to rehearse important sequences, such as counting and the days of the week, as well as taught rehearsal as a strategy. This helps to explain why, at one time tables were chanted by classes of young children. An example of group rehearsal.

The third lesson from memory studies is that children grow in their awareness both of themselves and of the ways of the world. They get better at spotting when they need to make an effort to remember. They also have a better understanding of what it is to 'forget'. This type of knowledge is called metamemory and is generally fully developed by the age of ten. Individual differences in memory are very considerable and therefore different people develop diverse approaches to the same task. This is particularly true of mental arithmetic. One important finding is that not only do children benefit from being taught strategies but this is enhanced if they are given feedback, e.g. 'You did so much better when you whispered those names over and over. I guess that helped you remember the pictures better' (Kennedy and Miller 1976). Even within the area of visual memory there is development. Adults scan complex pictures far more efficiently than five-year-olds. They have a richer store of images that is better organised (Mackworth and Bruner 1970). 'Regardless of the way that the information is presented, eight-year-old children tend to construct holistic representations of information that represents the important semantic relations in the information' (Paris and Mahoney 1974).

For all of us, changes in the way we organise our memories occur continuously in response to experience, particularly at the point that we attempt to recall them. Developmentally, by the age of ten, the underlying structure of memory is complete, although varying in important ways between individuals and between the sexes. An unpublished survey by one of the authors and a teaching colleague at a local secondary school gave the full adult picture of memory. There was also clear evidence of the problems created in our educational process by the dominance of verbal learning. The only difference between the high-achieving and low-achieving pupils was on their reported experience of verbal memory. Both groups used rehearsal to the same extent but the high achievers were seven times more likely to remember telephone and pin numbers, dates, lists and names.

Pupils may do well at school because they have good verbal memories. This matches the examination system but is not in itself an important long-term memory. It also biases learning towards females. For all pupils, there is a neglect of visual and practical learning. The load on memory for detail was also reflected in the fact that 70 per cent of the pupils reported difficulties in remembering 'things to take to school'. A similar percentage used 'other people' as their main external memory, usually 'mum'. Ninety-six per cent of all the students reported remembering things by 'pictures in the head'. This surprised their teachers who did nothing to encourage or develop this. Below are some remarks about their memories made by the pupils. Read them and see if you can relate them to the model of memory that we have been considering.

'I remember my form tutor in Year 8 because of the H Block fire.'

'The smell of grease reminds me of my Grandpa.'

'Every time I smell a certain smell I'm reminded of a box with the picture of a house on it.'

'I remember anything practical because I don't have to work anything out.'

'When I need to remember what homework I have, I picture what lesson I have on the day it was set.'

'I can picture a place but not the name of it. When I make arrangements to meet people we always describe it rather than name it.'

'I used to do this thing where I hold up a piece of paper above my head and I have to move my eyes up to see the word, and so in spelling if I was asked the word I would look up and remember it.'

'When I revise, I say key phrases and passages out loud and tape them and listen to it as I go to sleep.'

'If it's something dull and boring I'll have problems remembering it.'

'Because I enjoy these things, they are important to me, exciting things – things where there is something in it for me.'

'I don't use any strategies – and that's why I'm in trouble.'

There is solid evidence that people best remember experience and knowledge (episodic and semantic memory) obtained between the ages of ten and thirty (Rubin and Rahhal 1988). Consistent with this developmental view, and other points about memory and learning made in this chapter, the primary years (Key Stages 1 and 2) should be seen as a period for developing skills, language, cognitive processes and the rudiments of knowing. They are not a time for effectively learning (remembering) large amounts of subject knowledge. This is a task for Key Stages 3 and 4.

Finally, let us return to the opening point of this chapter, namely that we have a number of different and distinct memories and that we vary as individuals in how good or poor we are with them. Needless to say, research into children shows the same picture. One child will be good at picturing and weak at naming, and will use imagery in preference to language, whereas the reverse will apply to another child. In research carried out in 1975, 255 five-year-olds were given eleven different memory tasks, from verbal memory (number recall), from semantic memory (story recall) and from visual working memory (picture recall). There proved to be only a small relationship between a child's performance on any two tasks. It was not possible to use a child's ability on one memory task to predict their perform-ance on any other. This is an important though neglected finding (Stevenson *et al.* 1975). It was confirmed by research reported in 1998 where, again, children's ability to picture information was found to be separate from their ability to verbally remember it (Pickering *et al.* 1998). When a child fails to remember, a teacher should first consider the way the child was given the information and look for alternative ways of presenting and organising it. More generally, information is better presented in a multi-memory (multimedia) way, thus allowing children to use their own preferred strategies. This approach should continue throughout the education process. Talk and chalk is not only the wrong vehicle for some learning, particularly practical and physical skills, but it also restricts all learning if not complemented by other media. Our intuitive conception of memory as a predominantly verbal unitary trait is wildly inaccurate and our preference for teaching through language fails to maximise the education of all children, particularly boys. Children should also be taught how to use their memories more effectively. There are many practical ideas in this book as to how this can be achieved.

Practice Paper

Learning physical skills
(Invited paper from Christina Zergaeng)

This is primary a matter for procedural memory in the area of body movement.

When performing a movement, we get kinaesthetic feedback from our muscles and other parts of our body, which will eventually produce a movement 'memory' that will help us to know when an action 'feels' right. A new physical skill, such as driving a car, involves a lot of verbal cognitive thought processes to help us achieve the right actions, but as we practise more and become more skilled, our actions become automatic, hence the sensation of not remembering driving to work! Only in more difficult situations, such as a new traffic hazard, do we need to think consciously again about the task, i.e. we make our verbal memory attend to what we are physically doing, attend to our procedural memory. Through our verbal memory we also bring in our semantic and episodic memories.

In teaching a new movement skill, we want the child to experience the correct movement sequence for an action so as to get the correct sense of the movement in the body, and thus a correct physical memory of the action. The action 'feels' right and will eventually become automatic. There are different ways of helping the child to achieve this.

Learning by doing
Certain physical skills, such as learning to ride a bike, can be learnt by physically doing the task with support. This will either be stabilisers, or someone running behind holding the bike! The child gets the feedback from their legs, back and eyes that a certain way of riding the bike 'feels' right. Once this action is practised, the movement memory appears very strong, and once learnt, is rarely unlearnt. With practice, the action of riding becomes automatic. Cyclists rarely consider what they are doing when riding.

Multi-memory learning in physical skills
Most physical skills will be learnt with the use of a variety of our memories. Not only movement (procedural) memory is involved but also our understanding (semantic) as well as our visual and verbal processes. Feedback will generally be physical or kinaesthetic, but can be enhanced by the use of other memories:

Visual

Watch someone else perform the action → imitate it → feel what this is like physically → the feel of the action becomes the motor memory. This can be enhanced by using mirrors to give visual feedback. Picturing an action can also help you to remember the sequence of actions and perform better.

Verbal

Listen to verbal instructions → follow them to perform the task. This is likely to be helped by using verbal memory to rehearse the instruction while carrying out the movement sequence, e.g. 'hand up, back and throw'. Again, the objective is to get the 'feel' of the action, which will become the motor memory. Verbal directions play a significant part in the rough shaping of physical skills, as can be seen by words such as 'bend', 'reach', 'pull', 'thread', etc. that refer to actions.

Movement

The physical skill can be learnt by physically taking someone through the action. The use of picturing and talking through the sequence may enable the person to rehearse and practise the skill once they have been taken through the actions. Generally, procedural (movement) memory will be produced by performing the action. This memory will become stronger through practice and remove the need to picture and talk through. We often call this stage 'doing things automatically'.

Writing

In the initial stages of learning to write, the teacher gives the child a variety of prompts:

- visual – shows the child the formation of the letter on the board, in the air;
- verbal – talking the action through: h = 'down up and over';
- movement – hand over hand, taking the child through the action.

The teacher needs to get the child to imitate the action, by visualising (picturing) the action, and/or by repeating 'talking through' (verbal prompt), to achieve the correct movement.

At this stage, children are often concerned only with the end result, e.g. whether it looks like an 'a'. The teacher needs to ensure that the child realises that it is the sequence of actions that is important. Once a motor skill becomes automatic, it is hard to unlearn it. Hence children should not be allowed to practise the 'wrong', i.e. ultimately inefficient, way of writing the letters.

Sport skills

Sports teachers use all forms of prompts and feedback to help with the correct patterns of movement learning. It is important, especially for those who have difficulty in this area, to break the skill down into its constituent parts before building it up. Sports teachers know that the benefit of practice is that the skill becomes automatic, thus freeing the mind for thoughts of tactics and strategy.

Learning to type

Touch typists rely on their movement and visual spatial memories to 'know' where the letters are on the keyboard. Letter groups that are common, e.g. 'ing', are remembered as a movement sequence. Computer programs that teach touch-typing use a multi-memory approach to teaching movement skills. One such program (Mavis Beacon Teaches Typing) uses:

1. the movement memory of the fingers as they move from key to key, and the 'feel' of the home keys;
2. a visual image of the hands on the keys at the bottom of the computer screen (this is removed once the typist becomes more skilled);
3. advocating that the learner says each letter as they type it to reinforce which letter is being typed;
4. instant feedback in the form of the correct letter, or a noise if an incorrect letter is produced.

As we know, it takes a lot of practise to become a skilled touch typist, but once learnt, it is rarely forgotten.

Visualisation (picturing)

Some sports coaches encourage their pupils to visualise the skill that they are practising, and this appears to carry over into the physical skill when it is practised for real. This may be a useful strategy for children with weak verbal, but relatively good visual, recall.

Re-learning movement skills following injury

People who have suffered a severe head injury may lose physical skills and need to be re-taught. In some cases their movement memory appears partially to remain, and they may forget that they can't walk and first lurch themselves forward and fall on the ground.

Re-learning walking is taught by a skilled physiotherapist who is careful to ensure that the correct pattern and sequences of movement are recovered. Use of mirrors is helpful for children whose kinaesthetic feedback is impaired. Aids such as walking frames are helpful to support the child in correct movement patterns.

While a skill such as walking is being re-learnt, it requires the child's full attention, and thus the child is unable to walk and talk at the same time. It must be remembered that any child learning a new movement skill will require verbal prompts that are short and to the point, so that the child does not need to give too much attention to working out the verbal content. Many children find a mnemonic very helpful in remembering the correct sequence of actions.

Practice Paper

Visual shorthand

This is a term we have coined for the process of making personal notes and reminders by using quick iconic drawings. As far as we are aware, the approach is only found in an educational context in the work of Jem Long. Jem is a graphic artist and teacher who has already developed a unique early reading approach, published by Ginn, which integrates visual strategies in a play-reading format. Jem teaches in a Key Stage 2 speech and language unit and has taught his pupils to make a record of the instructions that they have to follow by making quick drawings. He also uses this approach to help his pupils remember what is going to happen and what is expected of them. Before discussing the method and its possible applications, we have reproduced some examples of the records made by his pupils (see Figures 1.3 and 1.4).

The pupils are given the instructions and record them using visual shorthand. Even when there is a significant time delay, during which the pupils do something else, they can follow their 'notes' easily.

Example 1
Instructions
First, will you do the two times table. When you have finished that, go and get your lunch box. Then go and wash your hands. When you have done that, we are going to sit down and share our snacks. After you have had your snack, we are going to listen to Lesley reading a story.

Figure 1.3 The 'notes' of three pupils

Example 2
Instructions
Take the key and unlock the grey cupboard. Get the musical instruments box out of the cupboard and then lock the cupboard up. On your way back to the classroom go into the office and pick up the register. While you are in the office, ask Mrs Dines to ring your mum and tell her that you are feeling better. Take the musical instruments back to the classroom. By then it will be home time, so you can put your chair on the table.

Figure 1.4 The 'notes' of three pupils

The most important point about visual shorthand is that the drawings are self-generated mnemonics for reminding yourself what to do. They are not designed to communicate to other people. As you know what you were thinking when you drew them, they, in turn will trigger your individual memory of the instruction or brief. None of the above examples can be worked out by a third party and we all need to know what the original instructions were to appreciate the effectiveness of the drawings.

Jem emphasises that the key to visual shorthand is learning the skill of answering the question 'what image will I require to remember this?'. The drawings are also not executed to be appreciated aesthetically by other people. Their artistic merit is irrelevant, provided that they point to their meaning for the individual who drew them. Drawing is seen today exclusively as art, when in fact it is a fundamental means of expressional communication that can be developed to a serviceable level in nearly everyone. Young children convey their understanding of the world around them through drawings, which can contain greater depth of meaning than they could express in speech alone. This early competence and confidence is often lost through neglect. For some individuals, particularly males, it is a strong area of individual strength that leads to educational disadvantage if they cannot use it. Visual shorthand could be taught to all pupils so that they could individually decide whether and when to use it.

The potential of visual shorthand has barely been explored; there is a long way to go before it is part of the educational culture. The example instructions above are extremely difficult to remember without making use of some sort of external memory. If unable to do so, many individuals would visualise themselves following out the instruction as a way of helping them remember. In other words, they would construct some sort of visual memory internally. This would probably be closely networked to keywords and phrases. This is the classic picture of our working memory in operation. In psychological terms, the central executive is combining information in the sketchpad and phonological memories. Trying to write down a full instruction would take significantly longer than drawing. Making a record using keyword and phrase notes would need to be practised by primary age pupils, who would also need to be fully confident and skilled phonic, even if not accurate, spellers. The examples show that no instruction is too complex to be treated in an iconic way. Clearly, self-generated icons can be combined with the writing of key words to construct notes. Keywords are particularly helpful for identifying the action needed, i. e. thread, pump, wrap, etc.

The skill of visual shorthand is fun to learn. The adult game of Pictionary shows one way in which the ability can be practised. Players of this game will also appreciate the communicative power of icons. They will also be aware that individuals vary in how good they are at constructing and interpreting icons, although we can all improve through teaching and practise.

Jem's approach has already begun to spread. A local secondary school has an attached facility for pupils with severe difficulties with literacy. One of the authors wrote the following consultation record on a Year 7 pupil in the facility.

Discussion

John's records show severe language processing difficulties. This includes word-finding problems. We need to find the sounds of the words in our heads in order to think in words. This makes John very visually dependent. Language can wash over him. He has currently given up searching for meaning in the speech that he hears. It is clear from reports about him, and from working with him that John does have a good semantic memory. His understanding is far better than he can indicate through writing and talking. Work with John shows that he already has an ability to use icons (quick drawings) to represent ideas, thoughts and knowledge.

Actions

1. John to practise making icons (for his own reference only). He needs to keep with him at all times a small plain-paper notebook.

2. All material to be keyworded using underlining, highlighters or through the notes of his in-class helper. Some keyworded material to be represented iconically. Known terms can be drawn by John, with new terms being drawn by the helper.

3. Very picturable stories to be used with John to reawaken his attempts to picture the language he hears. Once he has 'got' this we need to encourage him to re-listen in class.

4. Be aware of new objects in his school experience to label with words and icons, i.e. Bunsen burner, plane, squash racket, etc. Learning the verbal label for new objects is very hard for John, as even common word labels he can temporarily forget (not 'find').

Although not in the original consultation record, it is necessary to clarify how John's level of ability with icons was established. This was simply done by explaining what they were, demonstrating them and then asking him to draw some. A key finding was that when John was shown an example of an icon for an idea, instead of copying it, unprompted, he drew his own version. For example, John was shown the icon for 'ringing someone'.

 He drew:

Later in the assessment John neatly illustrated Jem's point that an icon is a trigger, a reminder, not a literal 2D representation and does not have to be accurate. John was asked to draw 'Get a Bunsen burner, tripod and u tube'. He drew the following

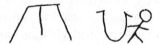

At first sight it looks as if he has forgotten to draw the Bunsen burner. Indeed that is what we concluded and asked him about it. He had drawn the Bunsen burner as being in the middle of the tripod, thus reducing the tripod to two legs. As he drew it, he will remember what the illustration is and this is its only purpose.

Visual shorthand has a wide range of uses. It plays a part in diagrammatic (mind mapping) approaches to note-taking at all levels. See the Practice Paper on Note-taking in Chapter 2. A well-known special needs strategy at primary level is the use of what are generally referred to as story boards, to lay out ideas in a sequence. This is used for children with very poor writing ability.

Pupils are expected to draw a series of scenes and there is always the spoken, or unspoken, assumption that the picture will communicate, even if only to the adult immediately involved. Using story boards and writing frames iconically extends their use as far as essay planners for Key Stage 4 pupils.

Acknowledgement
Thanks to Jem Long for his inspiration and his help in writing this practice paper.

Practice Paper **Differentiation and keywording**

In considering semantic memory we have already ascribed to it the role of understanding. We have also showed that its primary structure is one of icons (imagery) and word meanings. Knowing the meanings of words is one very clear way of representing the 'knowing that' type of knowledge that dominates school learning. When a teacher sets out to teach a lesson, they can start by asking themselves two questions: what new words do I want the pupils to learn the meaning of? and what words do I want them to develop the meaning of?, i.e. I might not know the meaning of the word 'gravity' or I might know something about the meaning but could learn more about its attributes. This isn't a usual starting place for teachers. The value of thinking in this way can, however, be seen more clearly when considering the topic of differentiation.

When children have learning difficulties, the task of the teacher is to differentiate the curriculum. Examining practice in this area shows that teachers set out to simplify what they want the pupils to learn. In doing so, they identify key concepts that they want to ensure that all the children understand. This is the same as identifying key words of which they want their pupils to learn the meaning. Differentiated material often presents these keywords in a diagrammatic and iconic context, i.e. the 'worksheets' use words and phrases linked and grouped by images and lines. Commonly, pupils for whom the material has not been prepared ask to use it because they find it easier to understand. What the teacher has done by producing differenti-ated material is in fact to communicate much more directly with all children's semantic memory and thereby make it easier for all pupils to understand the key ideas. This ensures that the teacher has at least established basic understanding in all pupils, and can hope for further understanding in some of the pupils because of the learning possible in the remaining lesson content. It is therefore good practice in all teaching to identify a core of key concepts (word meanings) and to present these in a diagrammatic and iconic form to all pupils.

Keywording as a skill features a great deal in this book. It is growing practice in learning support work in secondary schools. As we will see later, it can be taught to pupils. It is, however, vital that teachers first learn to use keywording themselves as a basis for their teaching goals. In terms of the curriculum, this needs to be done in a planned way but matters most at the level of individual lessons. The following is a list of teaching practices with respect to keywording:

1. When preparing a lesson, identify the key concepts in terms of keywords. At the very least give pupils a list of the keywords. You could also do the following (set out in priority order):
   a. Show the relationship between the key words by linking them in a simple diagram (mind map).
   b. Provide a definition of each word.
   c. Alongside each definition provide a simple icon (see the Practice Paper on keywords and icons for further details). You will probably need to draw these yourself at present. If you do, keep them in a subject department file so that you and other staff can use the same one in future.
   Alternatively, persuade your school to employ a graphic artist to work directly with teachers on developing icons and mind maps. If this isn't possible, find the 'visual thinkers and representers' on your own staff – look first in the Art, Technology and Geography departments. See if their time can be freed up to support colleagues.

2. When using textbooks, identify the keywords before the lesson. Start the lesson by getting the pupils to highlight, or underline in pencil, the keywords you have identified. Again, provide a simple diagram of them. When the pupils have built up experience of this they can then do their own diagrams of the identified words.

3. Use lists and diagrams of keywords as outline briefs for home-work or test revision.

4. Press within your school for keywording to be a central part of teaching and learning policy and practice.

Keywords and icons

In our earlier discussion of semantic memory, we identified links between keywords and visual images as being the primary content. This memory, in an educational context, we call understanding. Throughout this book you will find that keywords figure prominently. In this section we want to build on the link between keywords and images. In our semantic memory these links are rich, fluid and complex. However, it is possible to capture these in a way that allows the meaning of words to be suggested. A constructed image that suggests meaning is called an icon.

As I am word processing this, I can see displayed icons for cut, paste, open a file, print, text alignment, e-mail and many others. Computers now make extensive use of icons because of the ease with which they engage with our mental processes. This is discussed later in the section on IT. Icons can be constructed easily. They are never definitive; as we have seen this is not in their nature, but they prompt meaning. When we first look at a new icon on the computer we may guess straight away what it relates to, but we are more likely to need to trigger its function before we can see why the icon has been constructed in the way that it has. After we have learnt what it represents, the icon continues to act as a reminder of the function. Icons can be constructed for any area of human understanding. They are difficult to construct for abstract concepts and often take ingenuity, as well as assuming existing understanding (semantic memory) in the individuals whom you hope will find them helpful. If new understanding is primarily about remembering the meanings of new keywords, then iconic representations of this meaning have a vital role to play. We set our illustrator the challenge of constructing icons for randomly selected, difficult terms, found in GCSE textbooks. We argue that such books should make extensive use of icons. So should many dictionaries and encyclopaedias. This dream could well be realised through classroom Internet access to such reference material. At this level, one would expect that the icons would need to be constructed professionally. Textbooks could be following this practice now, using graphic artists to illustrate new terms. Figure 1.5 shows the icons that Ben constructed. Having drawn the icons, Ben made the following comments:

'I have always communicated using pictures, whether it be trying to get someone to remember a band name or offering directions. Being dyslexic myself, I have hugely enjoyed being involved with this fascinating project.

'When I first started sketching the icons for this book, my six-year-old nephew asked me what I was doing. I showed him the roughs for the 'Genetics' icon and explained (loosely) what genetics is. Two weeks later Jake was watching me preparing the finished icons and suddenly pointed to one of my illustrations and said "That's genetics, that is." If I needed any more proof that this system worked, that was it for me.

'This whole project has helped me understand more about my memory and the way I think. I believe that this method of icons could really open up a whole new way of working and learning for children and adults alike.'

Figure 1.5 Icons

Illustrations of this type are not used, because in our society images are used to entertain not inform. Learning is seen to be about the display of meaning through verbal means. The mastery of spoken and written language has the highest status, and the use of our education system to select those with the best abilities in these areas lingers on. Due to the status of words, illustrations are considered to be necessary only for the weak. But all children, and this includes those who are very able with words, would benefit from the wider use of icons. Those more dependent on their visual memories would understand and remember far more. You will recall from our earlier discussion that, in the human being, visual memory is more fundamental, with a greater capacity and more reliable access, than verbal memory. As it is strong in all of us, it should be the basis of our education system, not simply a support for those who are failing. Increasingly, those pupils who are struggling are being recognised and are receiving more attention. This is carried out under the heading of differentiation. Textbooks written for these pupils make much greater use of keywords, diagrams and illustrations. Although this is a move in the right direction, it does continue the association with special needs. In addition, the process lacks rigour, and is being done without a full awareness of the rationale and without the active interpretation of a graphic artist. All too often the illustrator is simply given a simple brief by the author. Icons communicate independently of spoken language and hence are truly universal. This is reflected in warning signs such as those for radiation and electricity. Looking to the future, the widespread use of standard icons on a medium such as the Internet could create an international symbol system. The starting point would be the iconic representation of all scientific and technical vocabulary.

Iconic support is increasingly used in special needs teaching, and the best developing practice can be found among those who teach language-impaired children. Language limitations are now seen as the fundamental characteristic of the majority of mainstream pupils with special needs. This is discussed further in Chapter 2. We would argue that low achieving children are largely also struggling with a mismatch between the language demands of the teaching and their own language ability. Special needs staff are increasingly devising their own icons to help pupils learn. If they can do it, so can all teachers. Good practice in subject teaching, despite the absence of the right textbooks, would mean teachers clearly identifying new terms and then illustrating them with their own icons. Subject departments in secondary schools could devise course summaries for students that consisted of the key terms with both verbal and iconic definitions. They would quickly find that their pupils understood and remembered better.

Through experience, teachers of young children have made extensive use of pictures and illustrations. Icons are used in ICT software programmes for pupils at Key Stages 1 and 2, and are used widely in computer games. In school learning, they are otherwise completely absent and they are rarely used even in special needs teaching at this level. The learning of any new vocabulary can be aided by using icons. Where there are keywords there can be icons. Artistic merit is irrelevant beyond the need to point to meaning. This is explored in our Practice Paper on visual shorthand earlier in this chapter.

Memory and Information Communication Technology

The fundamental nature of the link between ICT and memory can be seen by considering what lies behind the process of computers becoming user-friendly. Computers were considered to be hard to use; changes have been made and they are now less so. The changes have largely been in the way that computers interact with our memory processes. Computers used to be operated by the user recalling sequences of verbal codes. Not only was the user dependent on recall but the emphasis was entirely on the individual's verbal memory. This approach survives at MS.DOS level. The computer presents a blank screen, and codes are typed in to trigger responses from the computer. When the screen contains material, this is also altered by tapping keys in a remembered sequence. At this point, movement memory can begin to support verbal memory by storing a body memory for common typing sequences. The move to user friendliness has been a move towards engaging with the user's visual memory, particularly through recognition rather than recall. On a modern computer, choices are presented using little symbols and words right across the screen. In terms of memory, a visual field is simultaneously presented. Choices are made by recognising items on the field and then by moving another visual symbol, the cursor, over them. Not only are icons, i.e. images that suggest meaning, much in evidence, hence engaging visual recognition, but the screen is also made to work three dimensionally by using overlapping fields or windows. ICT has become user-friendly by moving from a verbal memory basis to a visual one. It will not have escaped the reader's attention that this is a move that the authors would like to see taking place within the education process itself. Indeed, the increased use of ICT as a teaching vehicle is strongly recommended since it facilitates a more effective engagement with the memory of the pupils being taught.

In a day-to-day practical context, the following uses of ICT to support memory have been observed to be effective.

1. A very poor movement memory can impair handwriting. Keyboard movements for typing the letters are much easier than the movement patterns for letters. Touch typing is not appropriate, as somebody with a poor movement memory needs visual monitoring of movements, i.e. they have to look at what they are doing.

2. Spelling is a difficult sequential memory. By word processing, rather than writing, spellings can be checked using the spelling memory in the computer.

3. When asked to reveal what you know about a topic, by either speaking or writing about it, the verbal memory is used to organise and sequence what you say/write. It stores important points until you have expressed them. It also organises the sentence structure for you and makes sure it is grammatical. This can all be done through word processing. The procedure is as follows:
    a. Type in any individual words about the subject that occur to you, regardless of the order in which they come into your head. Type them as a list – pressing *enter* after each one.

b. Use *cut and paste* to change the order of the keywords in your list until you have a sensible sequence of points.

c. Expand each keyword into a full sentence. You may find that you are combining keywords or that you are typing in more than one sentence.

d. Read through and alter, edit and expand.

You now have an essay, or account, that has been constructed using the computer to replace operations that you would have otherwise carried out in your own short-term verbal memory.

4. There are computer programs that allow the substitution of icons for words. These can be used to help pupils construct an account or to give access to text.

5. Increasingly, computers are available in schools with adequate voice recognition to allow text to be generated from speech. This allows a way of permanently recording information currently in verbal memory, i.e. it provides a very good external memory alternative. More available are text readers that speak text to the user. This allows access to this external memory. The use of this form of external memory can also be used to supplant short-term verbal memory when constructing an account.

6. ICT software increasingly contains unlimited external memories for the individual. The Internet itself represents one vast memory.

Chapter 2

Memory and language

In this chapter, we look more closely at the link between verbal memory and the learning and use of language. We have already seen that semantic memory offers keywords and images and associations. These are structured, organised and systematically represented by language. Our verbal memory plays a key part in this process. It also plays a key role in our learning of language in the first place. The phonological and verbal aspects of memory are looked at with the language-impaired and with the hearing-impaired. From this there are implications and strategies to consider. Within this context the term 'hearing-impaired' describes pupils with hearing loss ranging from moderately to profoundly deaf, who have an auditory–oral method of communication and education.

Verbal working memory refers to the brief amount of time that we can hold on to information after we have perceived it. Information held here decays within two seconds unless it is verbally rehearsed by 'speaking to oneself'. The speed of our inner articulation determines how much language/information we can hold in this two-second slot. The ability to rehearse is present from at least three years old (Gathercole and Adams 1993). The ability to deliberately rehearse doesn't emerge until about seven years old (Gathercole *et al*. 1994), although, as Chapter 1 showed, it is a skill that younger children can be taught. The memory span refers to the number of items or units of information that can be stored within this two-second slot before being lost, e.g. how many words or numbers can be recalled. This amount of information (i.e. the span) increases as children grow up. The increase is due to the increasing speed with which one speaks to oneself and the speed with which one removes words from the slot, i.e. as vocabulary and grammar improve. There are considerable individual differences in this memory. These seem to be primarily due to rehearsal–speed variations.

The term 'phonological loop' refers to the temporary storage of the verbal/phonological information perceived within this brief two seconds by verbal rehearsal. We need to temporarily retain information in the short-term store for long enough to be able to make sense of the whole of the message. This can then be transferred to long-term semantic memory. A further illustration of why we require this skill is seen in the need to remember information from the beginning of a sentence (spoken or read) for long enough to make sense of the whole sentence. As we use this memory when speaking and writing sentences, it is also critical in helping to make our constructions grammatical.

Verbal rehearsal is the strategy we use to increase the time in which we hold information in the short-term store. This extra time may allow us to go into another room and still recall a new telephone number before dialling it. It may also enable a child, through the verbal repetition of the sentence they have just heard, to gain time to have another chance to process its meaning, or to retain what they are trying to write during the time that they are writing it.

Verbal rehearsal to oneself is often referred to as *inner speech*. Research emphasises the role of verbal working memory, inner speech development, sub-vocalisation (silent movement of the speech muscles) and speaking out loud in developing literacy as well as speech (Baddeley 1986). Lane (1981) developed ARROW as a strategy for children with reading and spelling difficulties, using a tape recorder to enable children to record and listen to their own voice. This is a multi-memory rehearsal strategy.

Aural	child listens to speech on headsets
Read	child listens to the voice as they read corresponding material–visual support
Responds	child speaks and imitates
Oral	child repeats the model and listens to his/her own recorded voice replayed
Written	child writes from his own voice recording.

Lane highlighted the value of self-voice in developing reading both with hearing and hearing-impaired children. Tape recorders and camcorders are now being used to help hearing-impaired children develop language and literacy processing skills (such as re-telling and writing a story), and tape recorders are being used to help children with specific language impairment to develop phonological reading skills through the use of self-voice. Jenny Jones details this in her Practice Paper in Chapter 3 on supporting verbal working memory.

First, a brief overview of how the verbal working memory relates to and affects language development, language processing, and literacy with the hearing.

Language development

Initially, the phonological system begins to develop (i.e. learning and recognising the speech sound patterns of the language). Research suggests that children's phonological memory skills (verbal working memory) predict their ability to learn new sound patterns (Gathercole 1990). The child's vocabulary develops as first words are understood. Verbal working memory has been shown to relate to children's ability to learn new words (ibid.).

The syntactic system (the grammar and structure of the language) begins with word combinations, and progresses to complex multi-clause sentences. It is difficult to see how someone can recall, process and understand the meaning of a long complex embedded sentence without the use of a functional verbal working memory, e.g. 'The boy who didn't show up for practice wasn't allowed to play on the team until a week later' (CELFR Semel *et al.* 1987). Pupils with a severe verbal working memory difficulty are unlikely either to use or recall sentences using language structures of this length and complexity (Gathercole and Baddeley 1993).

Language processing

Language processing is a prerequisite for coping and succeeding in schools, as spoken language is the medium used to convey most of the teaching. From Year 2 onwards, learning is currently primarily a verbal experience and the curriculum is linguistically based.

Language processing depends on the interrelationship between verbal memory and language. In listening, a child has to process the vocabulary and the sentence structure to grasp the meaning of what is being explained. Verbal working memory is needed to hold on to the individual words, before the explanation can be understood and then stored in long-term semantic memory. If the vocabulary is difficult, if the sentence structure is too complex for the child's language development, and if the sentence is too long for the child to remember all that was said while trying to reach the meaning, then overload is experienced. Of the information to be conveyed there may be only partial sense made and stored, the first or last words in the sentence absorbed, or frequently no details at all conveyed and retained.

The difficulties faced in school range from reception age children listening to a new story to secondary age students being given complex instructions and explanations in a science lesson. Strategies such as rephrasing instructions and explanations to an appropriate language level (chunking sentences) can increase the opportunity for participation in the classroom.

Literacy development

Current research into literacy development has focused on the strong association of phonological awareness with reading ability (Gathercole 1990). That is, children's ability to recognise and discriminate between sounds in words has been linked to the development of reading. Children with difficulties in recognising and distinguishing between the sounds in the words they hear will have difficulties with the word in written form. Instead of phonological awareness there is phonological confusion. Trying to relate graphemes (letters) to sounds when there is such confusion over the sound to be represented would seem to be an impossible task for these children. Following this area of research, there has begun a retrieval of the lost oral tradition within early years teaching, with singing and chanting of songs (rhymes and patterns of sounds including rhythm), which help develop inner voice and support phonological (verbal) memory and phonological awareness.

Verbal working memory correlates with individual differences in reading ability but not to the same extent as phonological awareness. Phonological awareness is more strongly associated with reading ability, than verbal working memory. However, Gathercole (1998) suggests two-way feedback between phonological memory and phonological awareness.

There are further developments looking at this area in relation to early reading skills, such as PhAB (the Phonological Assessment Battery) devised to look at children's difficulties with phonological awareness (Frederickinson *et al.* 1997). Also PAT (Phonological Awareness Training) (Wilson 1993 and 1994), devised as a programme for children with phonological difficulties in reading and spelling using onset and rime, i.e. shout: sh (onset) out (rime). The tape-recording approach using self-voice feedback and writing is being used successfully to help those children experiencing great difficulty with phonological awareness and verbal working memory.

Literacy processing

Reading for meaning and understanding involves the combination of semantic memory, language development, language experience and verbal working memory. If the vocabulary is unfamiliar, the syntax is too difficult, or the load on memory too high, the child may decode the print with accuracy but without understanding (barking at print). This is critical where the text gives opportunities for deductive information which has to be stored, put together and analysed to give the correct answer to questions.

For example:
I have wings and fly and I nest in trees.
What am I?
I have wings and fly and I carry people.
What am I?

To make sense of what has just been read, all of the information has to be recognised and retained to be put together. Children who do not store and process all of the information presented will not make good sense of what they appear to read with accuracy. They may be unable to use the information in the last part of the description to help distinguish between the two descriptions. Assumptions can never be made about a child's processing and understanding. 'I have wings and fly and I carry people. What am I?' A recent response to this was 'God'. These difficulties are further explored in the reading comprehension Practice Paper later in this chapter.

Writing and processing skills

Verbal memory is a necessary component in the production of written work as well as in the development and processing of language and literacy. The frequently occurring situation in the classroom is that of being presented with information in spoken or written form and being required to write about it, or even retell it in written form. For example, being asked to retell a story involves having to process the language, store the meaning and organise the ideas for retelling while grappling with the movement task of writing, while trying to remember how to spell the words. Not surprisingly, a common outcome is that ideas are lost (forgotten) in the complex effort to remember. Practical strategies for students with severe memory problems like this are looked at in later Practice Papers and in Chapter 1 (visual shorthand). Tape recorder and camcorder work is being used with hearing-impaired children, to help in the development of narrative skills (spoken and written).

Difficulties are also apparent when the task involves any form of dictation. As a teacher rapidly imparts the homework to be done, those children with memory problems are likely to recall only part of a lengthy sentence to write down, and more may be lost in the effort of writing, when at home no one, child or parents, can deduce what it was that was required. On the whole it is now recognised that good practice in the classroom involves homework being clearly presented visually, with adequate time being allowed to copy this if required. In addition, teachers need to be aware of which students require homework to be written into their books for them. However, difficulties in this area continue to commonly occur.

The language-impaired

We have already seen that language delay can be strongly linked to limitations in working verbal memory. There is a large group of children whose delay and confusion over speech and language is such that they are identified as having language impairment. Estimates of the number of children who should be considered as belonging to this group vary, but a generally agreed figure is between five and ten per cent. Every teacher will regularly have to teach a language-impaired child. This is a complex area of need, as children can have difficulties with understanding, speaking clearly, speaking in sentences or in using language. Types of difficulty can be broken down further, and indeed have to be, when helping the children to develop their missing skills. Do these children have anything in common? Among professionals working with these children it is a standard experience that, as a group, they have poor verbal working memories, often referred to as auditory memory. A number of studies have shown beyond any doubt that what distinguishes language-impaired children is their poor verbal working memory (Bishop *et al*. 1996). Typically the performance of all the language-impaired children is worse than all the other children that they are compared to. This is such a clear result that Bishop, North and Donlan propose that it is the very best way of identifying a language-impaired child. Previously Bishop had found that language-impaired children had all the characteristics that we can now clearly see as consequences of a poor verbal working memory (Bishop 1992). They had normal understanding (semantic memory) but a poor vocabulary, set in short sentences which often included grammatical mistakes.

We are now going to attempt to briefly explore how a poor verbal working memory affects the learning of new words and how it limits sentences. The key fact is the too rapid disappearance of what has been heard. As the child looks around they hear the language of the adult that they are with. Gradually they work out how bits of what they hear (spoken words) relate to what they see. The same is true for all aspects of experience. Adults help the child do this by altering what they say and by pointing to certain objects. It is harder to link spoken words with your experience if the word is quickly forgotten. Learning proper nouns, such as people's names, and learning the names of the colours, is more difficult than learning common nouns, such as the names of objects, e.g. cup, towel, chair, etc. The fact that each person has their own name, and that there are hundreds of colour shades, means that the sound of the word has to stay around that bit longer if the correct connection is to be made. Children who are slow to learn the words for the colours and who have difficulty remembering peoples names nearly always turn out to have poor verbal working memories, although they may not noticeably be language-delayed or language-impaired. Teachers of young children should use poor knowledge of colour words as a warning of possible learning difficulties. It would be advisable to treat them as if they had poor verbal memories. This book has advice on how to do that.

With a poor verbal working memory, why is it hard to learn the grammar of long sentences and why is it hard to understand and speak and write such sentences, even when you know the grammar? The answer is a complex one but the following examples may illuminate:

1. *The lady who sits on the chair by the till is our teacher*

The basic sentence here is 'the lady is our teacher'. The sentence has been split and you have to store 'the lady' in verbal working memory while lots of other words are added. Typically, children with poor verbal working memories remember the core sentence and forget one or both of the additional clauses. Sometimes they use their semantic memory for 'lady' and as a result move away from the actual spoken word. They can then produce lady, woman, or other words of a similar meaning.

2. *It was dark as the wolves came up the road.*

In listening to sentences, and in producing them yourself, the appropriate tense is not always clear. If the sentence begins in a particular tense then it must also end in it. Pupils often make a mistake over the tense of a word because they have forgotten the tense it is in. In this example they have to remember that they used the word 'was', not the word 'is'. If they forget they may well say or write: 'it was dark as the wolves come up the road'.

As educational psychologists, we routinely meet children whose difficulties are traceable to an underlying deficit with verbal working memory. Below we have reproduced a case study. The individual is a girl. We pointed out in the very first paragraph of the book that females have a relative strength with language. This is reflected in the area of language impairment, where they only constitute approximately one in ten of the children identified. Janet (not her real name) was about to transfer to secondary school at the point when this assessment was made. Clear recommendations for teaching Janet emerge from the assessment.

As a preschool child, Janet was identified as having significant language and movement delay. Initially she received educational programmes at a Pre-School Centre as well as speech and language therapy. She transferred from there to an Infant Speech and Language Unit, then to the Junior Unit in the same school. Over the last year she has been integrated, with support full time into a mainstream Year 6 class. As a preschooler, Janet's language delay was traced to a very poor verbal working (phonological) memory (auditory memory). At the time of this assessment it was just being realised that this memory was the most fundamental influence on the acquisition of language. Janet was assessed using non-word repetition – the child repeats nonsense words: digit span – the child repeats numbers, e.g. 4, 2 and then 6, 9, 3. The child is asked to repeat longer and longer strings of numbers: sentence recall – the child repeats sentences, and the Token Test – this test begins by laying out in front of the child different sizes and shapes of coloured discs. Directions are then given by the person testing, e.g. 'Touch the big blue square with the small red circle'. Janet also had slow movement development. Developmentally, Janet has had substantial barriers to her effective learning and functioning. Thanks to the very good educational provision made and the excellent support from home, Janet has learnt language systems and processes. Similarly, she has acquired movement skills in those areas where she has had concentrated practise including handwriting.

In terms of her cognitive profile, Janet has severe deficits with procedural memory (body/movement memory) and verbal working memory. These memories constantly let her down and she has to continually work round the difficulties they pose. Janet has mastered important areas of coordination and movement, but in order to be effective she has to concentrate to a very high degree. So, for example, the effort she puts into her handwriting is considerable. Janet has developed an adequate vocabulary; she has also mastered sentence structure in both spoken and written language. However, Janet continues to fail to retain verbal information and to use her working memory effectively to organise her conscious thoughts, deliberate actions and her conversation and written communication.

With poor verbal memory, although the language is heard, it disappears extremely quickly. This memory is also used in an active way in order to structure our thinking in language, which is why it lies behind action planning, conversation and written responses in class. This memory deficit of Janet's is a constant barrier. She has to take information from this poor memory before it disappears. Janet has learnt to do this to a maximum extent by increasing the speed with which she removes items from her verbal memory and makes them meaningful. For example, where previously she scored poorly on the Token Test she now scores within the average range, and her success on this test derives from her speed of response. She rapidly converted verbal instructions into a plan of action and therefore there was much less need to retain what was said for further processing.

As well as speeding up how quickly she takes meaning away from what she hears, she has learnt a whole range, of strategies for coping with her memory difficulty. In more detail, Janet's problem with an extremely weak verbal memory affects the following areas:

- She forgets new detail and new information rapidly and finds it very hard to build this into her memory. Anything verbally new is very dependent on verbal memory.
- She very easily forgets important details, instructions, directions, guidelines and briefings about new situations or changes in familiar situations.
- She has difficulty in consciously organising her work and the sequence of actions or items required in order to express herself verbally, in writing or in a set of actions. Although she has plenty of meanings and a lot of understanding, her verbal memory structures these and gives direction and organisation. In themselves, Janet's very weak verbal memory and her poor movement memory will always be deficits which she will have to adjust to, work round and build into her strategies and preferences.

Although Janet has made progress in many areas of learning, such as word recognition and spelling, she constantly experiences a difficulty in functioning. This is made very clear by her class teacher who has got to know her well. Janet is described as having flashes of ability. She has very good artistic drawing and makes quick cartoons and diagrams. This is using her sketchpad (visual) memory strengths. Though she can reason out and assemble complex ideas, she then forgets the structure of these. Most noticeably in class, Janet has difficulty in remembering a new routine, procedure or activity, especially when this involves homework. In the classroom, Janet needs daily attention to help her organise her tasks and identify the framework within which she is working. Currently, one hour a day is used to help her organise her activity within the classroom, while a further hour is used for memory training. In Maths and in other practical areas, Janet can forget key procedures and sequences; these are again retained in verbal memory. Similarly, another characteristic of verbal memory is also noted, in that Janet finds it difficult to remember the new words for concepts that are taught in, for example, Science.

Janet's motivation and application is extremely high and she is hardworking and determined. Inevitably, however, her confidence can be shaken by the constant difficulty she encounters. She is only just beginning to develop an awareness of the nature of her difficulty and how it impacts on her functioning. She needs to learn a whole range of scripts that will make it clear to others what she finds difficult and how to help her. For example, 'Please say that again', 'Did you say ...'; 'I have a poor memory for what you say so please say it simply and repeat it'; 'can I tell you what I have to do so that you can see if I have got it right or not?' These scripts will be particularly important when Janet transfers to secondary school.

It is not helpful to seek to improve Janet's verbal memory directly, as this is not possible. She can only learn to use the capacity she has efficiently. This she is probably doing. The most helpful approach is for her to learn the sorts of sentences that are used to express knowledge in the different subjects. This familiarity with how things are said and written about in Science or in Geography will help Janet quickly take the meaning away from the sentences and reduce the load on her verbal memory. Currently, this is being done in the class by looking at the way mathematics problems are presented within language. Janet is being helped to rapidly deconstruct the maths problem language and identify the important parts to work on.

When she transfers to secondary school Janet will need daily contact with a personal teaching tutor in order to help her organise the new information she has received and to relate this to task assignments, particularly homework. Not only does Janet need to have a clear idea of what homework to do and when it needs to be handed in, but she also needs to be sure of what content is required. She needs to remember the right information from the lessons. Support for homework assignments is a very good focus at secondary level for bringing to the attention of the personal tutor the messages and contact required with subject teachers on her behalf. The personal tutor can then quite clearly see where particular strategies and approaches are needed to ensure that Janet has a better chance to identify missed information. In addition, the personal tutorial time will also serve to help her structure and identify information required. It may initially be necessary to do some home-work during this time.

The tutor will need additional time to liaise with subject teachers, other support staff and external therapists. The session would centre on difficulties in handling and identifying important information and how to record and use it. The personal tutor would also be responsible for maintaining a home–school liaison book, which would draw together any subject teacher comments. The home–school book would also contain observations and comments from home regarding Janet's difficulties with the school process. The personal tutor would then be in a position to respond to these and liaise with subject teachers.

If problems in subject lessons persist despite liaison and development of strategies, it may be necessary to put in individual support during some lessons.

The hearing-impaired

A focus on the hearing-impaired can help our understanding of the task facing all pupils, and the challenge posed to their teachers. The effect of phonological or verbal working memory on learning has also been considered with deaf and hearing-impaired students (Marschark 1993, 1998). It is also significant with the hearing-impaired in terms of:

- developing language;
- processing information in the classroom;
- developing literacy.

In an unpublished survey carried out by one of the authors (Bristow 1999) it was decided to look at a local population of hearing-impaired students. They ranged over the continuum from those needing unit support to those needing school for the deaf support. An attempt was made to look at working memory in a functional way. It was seen that

- hearing-impaired students could function in mainstream with major deficits in verbal working memory and language processing;

- auditory–oral hearing-impaired students have a range of verbal working memory skills;
- those with greater difficulties than other hearing-impaired students in functional verbal working memory are likely to have greater difficulties in processing information and in functioning in mainstream. Those with the greatest difficulties in functional verbal working memory had difficulties in progressing in auditory–oral schools for the deaf.

The functional assessment of verbal memory looked at pure verbal recall with recall of digits. Memory–language recall and processing was looked at with sentence and story recall. There was also a modified version of the story, with shorter modified language structures (chunked sentences). Sometimes students appeared unable to recall any of the story. However, when presented with the modified version sometime later, they could recall parts or even all of it. This gives some indication of the interrelationship between memory and language and also of how teachers can help students to access information by the use of modified language. Reading comprehension underpins understanding of much of the school curriculum. This was a further factor looked at. Its relation to memory and language processing can be seen in Figure 2.1.

On a functional level, at secondary transfer, sentence and also story recall appear to be critical factors in determining how hearing-impaired students progress and cope in mainstream. Some illustrations of the range of scores and the relatively low levels with which some students coped with mainstream classes are given in Figure 2.1). Some instances of hearing students in mainstream with difficulties in this area were also looked at.

Within every class there can be students with these kinds of difficulties, trying to process information, whether hearing-impaired or hearing. When teachers are able to take account of these difficulties, more students can be helped to gain access to the curriculum. With hearing-impaired students, as mentioned earlier, this difficulty in processing spoken information can be worked on through developing narrative skills:

- listening to stories;
- retelling stories;
- rewriting stories;
- going through the above sequence again and again – using tape-recorders or camcorders.

This is discussed later, in relation to strategies for developing descriptive writing.

Discussion of the student scores in Figure 2.1

The four students with hearing impairment show a range of scores representing a range of functioning across the continuum from mainstream unit to school for the deaf. The relative difficulties of all these students in recalling sentences are shown.

	Recall of digits span	Celf R Sentence recall raw score	Celf R (hearing norms)	Story recall	Reading compre-hension (hearing norms)
Case 1 Severe–profound loss					
Age 11y4 Yr 7	5 digits	48	(6y0)	9/11	9y4 – 10y11
Age 13y11 Yr9	6 digits (c = 50 av. H. norms)	52	(6y0 –11)	10/11	12y0
Case 2 Moderate–severe loss					
Age 11y7 Yr 7	4–6 digits (c= 14 low H. norms)	32	(<5y)	5/11	7y9 – 9y2
Case 3 Very severe–profound loss					
Age 11y5 Yr6		29	(<5y)	1/11	<7y0
Age 13y8	3–6 digits (c = 5 v. low H. norms)			6/11	8y6
Case 4 Profound–very profound loss					
Age 10y7	3 digits (c<1 v. Low H. norms)	1	(<5y)	1/11	<7y0
Age 11y8 Y6	3 digits max (c<1 H. norms)	Crystal Imitation 3 word utterance			
HEARING					
Case 5					
Age 12y3 Yr 8	3–4 digits v. low c = 1 H. norms	46	(5y0 – 11)	7/11	R.Comp 11y0 R. Acc 8y9 Spelling 7y0
Case 6					
Age 12y0 Yr 7		44	(5y0 – 5y11)	4/11	

Figure 2.1 The hearing-impaired

On entry to secondary school, even the first student is functioning around the six-year level according to hearing norms. The second and third students, typical of many hearing-impaired students, function in mainstream beneath the five-year level. Because of the relatively low levels at which the hearing-impaired students were functioning, it was found to be more helpful when looking at the range to look at raw scores with sentence recall.

The first student has competent processing skills. His ability to recall sentences, although low on hearing norms, reflecting the language delay in the hearing-impaired, is relatively high among the hearing-impaired. His pure verbal working memory was average in relation to hearing norms. He uses his competent verbal memory and his semantic and episodic memory to make sense of and to recall stories. His understanding of reading is sound. There are no major processing problems and he coped well with secondary school.

The second student started at secondary school with greater difficulty in recalling sentences, with a poor working memory (in recall of digits), with weak recall of story and weaker skills in reading comprehension. She needed a high level of support to cope with the secondary school curriculum. She had difficulty in processing spoken information and complex written information. She had great difficulty in producing written course work (a more advanced form of 'retelling a story').

The third student was a concern at junior school. In Years 4 and 5 he produced no written work in class that was not copied. This student's recall of sentences was at a lower level. His pure working memory with recall of digits was very low. He could not recall a short story. In class the explanation and discussion 'flew over his head' and was not processed by him. He needed focused work involving rehearsal and much repetition to develop his narrative skills to the stage where he could recall, retell and write out a 'story'. His teacher hit upon the following strategy:

1. He and his teacher read a known story together.

2. His teacher rewrote the story in modified language (chunked). He took this home and read it aloud to an adult every day for about four or five days.

3. After this consolidation he began to reread and retell the story to his teacher – with many repetitions (reading aloud and retelling).

4. He wrote the story out from recall – his first ever piece of written narrative.

He needed all the overt rehearsal (hearing his own voice reading aloud) and repeated repetition (allowing him to transfer more and more items of information into a growing whole in semantic memory, and finally allowing him to recall and organise his ideas so that he could retell them). If the research on verbal working memory, the value of self-voice and Lane's multi-memory approach had been known to us then, we could also have allowed this student the opportunity to listen to his own recorded voice as he reread the story, and to rewrite the story from his self-voice.

This student transferred to a secondary school for the deaf. His retelling of a story improved, even though his verbal memory remained a problem:

age 11y5	story recall	1/11
age 13y8	story recall	6/11

This student was able to learn rehearsal as a strategy, even at a fairly late age, and to use it to move on to develop language processing skills. When he was seen at 13y8 he was also able to write about what he had just read without difficulty.

The fourth student attended a school for the deaf. She had complex processing difficulties. Progress was very slow. She had great difficulty in recalling sentences with the sentence recall task. With Crystal's (1986) sentence imitation task she was recalling three-word utterances. As a sentence lengthened to 'He can see a cat and a dog', she went into overload. Her verbal memory was impaired, with memory span restricted to three digits. Language processing was a major difficulty.

Recall of a short story was not possible. Processing of more than three sequential verbal units of information was not possible (the request to touch the small yellow circle could be carried out; the request to touch the green square and the red circle could not because the sequenced units of information were too much for recall and processing).

This student found it harder to process sequenced pieces of information (such as a string of adjectives) than she did grammatical information. For example, she could correctly process a sentence such as 'Put the white circle in front of the blue square'. She could follow the instruction 'Pick up the squares, but not the yellow one'. Yet she could not follow a structurally simpler sentence such as 'Touch the green square and the red circle'. This student's difficulties are seen to lie with language processing rather than language acquisition: the language was all familiar.

When this student was given information that was supported by signs, her capacity extended beyond the three units. When she was given information that was chunked and supported by gesture she became more confident and relaxed. It was felt inappropriate to expect a student with these kinds of difficulties to rely purely on verbal instruction without strategies to support her recall, comprehension and expression.

The cognitive profile suggested that this student had procedural (movement) memory difficulties, with accompanying organisational problems, in addition to her hearing impairment and her verbal working memory difficulties. This made language processing very difficult and functioning within the classroom challenging, even within a school for the deaf. Multi-memory strategies like those mentioned above and the extensive use of visual cues and visual shorthand (Chapter 1) were all considered necessary to support these complex difficulties. In addition, this student needed help in developing movement memory.

As can be seen from the strategies raised above, meeting the special needs of hearing-impaired students with such additional complications raises issues within a wholly auditory–oral approach.

To be effective, strategies and support have to address children's needs in a multi-memory way. Hearing children with special educational needs (SEN) have better access to a multi-memory approach (when appropriate). Hearing-impaired children have an equal right to the opportunity to use these strategies. This is not implying a recommendation for a particular communication approach. These strategies are equally relevant in both auditory–oral and total communication/signing educational systems.

Figure 2.1 also contains data on two hearing students who were causing some concern at secondary school. The scores showed difficulties in similar areas.

The fifth student (see Figure 2.1) had difficulty in recalling sentences according to hearing norms. She also had significant difficulty with the recall of digits task. These scores suggest verbal working memory and processing problems. She was seen as a bright and able girl in school. She appeared able to read and understand her schoolwork. Her written work was poor; some staff thought she was just lazy or 'scatty'. She had covered up her major verbal working memory problems. Her parents were concerned over her spelling.

Further test results showed that, as well as having a severe verbal working memory problem, she had an accompanying phonological awareness problem and could not recognise 'rime' sounds as she listened to words. This relates to the earlier discussion in this chapter about phonological/verbal memory and literacy development. This difficulty resulted in her difficulty with spelling and her low reading accuracy score (reading decoding) in relation to her reasonable reading comprehension skills. This student was physically unable to take notes or take down dictation in class. She was trying to recall what she had heard, and, trying to spell it, she would go into overload and forget what she was trying to write. In this situation, the working memory difficulty is affecting a hearing student's functioning within the class and manifests as a specific difficulty in producing written language. Classroom management avoiding the need for dictation, and the development of more visual means of note-taking (see Chapter 1) would help this student to function more effectively at school.

The sixth case concerns a student with learning and organisational difficulties. This student was completing no written work in class and there was concern about her ability to follow verbal instructions. She had memory and processing difficulties. Her scores with recall of sentences and with story recall were in a similar range to the hearing-impaired students. In talking to this student and working with her, she told us about an incident; following this she wrote down everything about it without effort. When her bemused teacher pointed out that she had produced more written work now than in any lesson, even with a support teacher explaining to her what to write, she responded instantly, 'It was easy because I said it first'. When she was in class processing verbal information, she not only had difficulty in recalling what she had to do, but without saying it out loud, her inner voice was not sufficiently strong to be able to guide her in what to write.

This student not only needed visual cues and short chunked sentences for instructions, she also needed the opportunity to say her answer aloud to enable her to write it. This is not seen as an acceptable or often practical strategy within many secondary class-rooms. In this example the verbal memory-language processing difficulty manifests as a difficulty in following verbal instructions and a difficulty in producing or completing any written work.

The above examples indicate some ways in which verbal working memory and language processing can make it difficult, but not impossible, for students to succeed in the classroom. In any class there will be students with less severe problems, who will not necessarily be identified as having these processing difficulties and who will be helped by teachers using such strategies.

In our overview of memory and language we have so far concentrated on the nature of the connection between verbal memory and the learning and use of language. We have done this both by looking at the research and by considering the difficulties experienced by language- and hearing-impaired pupils as well as those with undetected verbal memory difficulties. We now need to remind ourselves of the original argument outlined in the first chapter. It is our contention that the demands on the verbal memories of pupils in our education system are extreme, and that many of them find their verbal memories inadequate to the task. Multi-media and multi-memory methods and practices will benefit all pupils and allow for the more successful inclusion of pupils with language and hearing impairment. Below is a series of Practice Papers that explore the problem areas and advance practical suggestions.

Acknowledgements to Honor Andersen, SEN Advisor for Specialisms, for her support and role in making the research with the hearing-impaired possible and fruitful.

Facilitating memory for language – a strategic approach
(Invited paper from Louise Kelly and Angela Belliveau)

Practice Paper

The following ideas were collated as a result of working with primary and secondary schools as speech and language therapists. In addition, we were invited to form part of a multi-disciplinary working party examining practical approaches to compensate for auditory (verbal working) memory impairment. This was an enlightening experience, which brought together a variety of different perspectives. Finally, ideas have been gained from attending study days about memory, notably, Jane Mitchell's course *Effective Therapy: Practical Applications of Memory Theory For Use With Dyslexic and Language Disordered Children* based at University College, London.

An overview of memory and language
Considering that language, learning and aspects of memory are so closely connected, there is a surprising lack of detailed information about memory and its link to learning language. In many speech- and language-related books and journals, verbal memory (memory for language that is heard) is often only mentioned in passing as a pre-requisite for learning language. Most teachers and speech and language therapists recognise the importance of verbal memory when learning language, and may have attempted to improve a child's verbal memory using various activities such as asking the child to follow instructions of increasing length (e.g. 'I went to market' etc.). Disappointment may then follow as it is discovered that the child continues to have difficulty in everyday situations. This can lead to a feeling that verbal memory cannot be improved. (We aim to demonstrate that strategies can improve how well you use your verbal memory.)

In other areas of literature, there is an abundance of information about memory techniques, claiming to enable people to pass exams more easily or to recall vast amounts of information. Jane Mitchell, a speech and language therapist and dyslexia teacher, has linked theories and memory techniques used by adults without language difficulties to therapy/teaching for adults and children with specific memory deficits. She believes that it is possible to improve a learner's memory by teaching them to use strategies. This is achieved by helping an individual to be aware of the techniques they are using when trying to remember something. This knowledge is then related to real-life situations. Jane Mitchell describes these ideas in more detail in her computer program *Mastering Memory* (1998), a computerised version of the therapy tool *Memory Bricks (Mitchell 1994)*.

There are various forms of memory and a number of models to describe the process of memory. Jane Mitchell describes memory as being divided into three stages:

1. acquisition – sometimes called *input* or *encoding* (how you take information in e.g. paying attention, senses);
2. retention – sometimes called storage or processing (what you do with the information to remember it);
3. retrieval – sometimes called *output* or *recall* (this involves recalling information, e.g. someone's name, subject specific vocabulary, an event or sequence of events).

Difficulties can occur at any stage of the memory process, and a breakdown at the level of acquisition or retention is likely to affect other stages. Memory is greatly influenced by a number of prerequisite factors, which should be considered before analysing the memory process. Jane Mitchell presents a comprehensive checklist of these factors, which include:

- satisfactory hearing and vision;
- ability to perceive the difference between sounds (e.g. hearing the difference between individual speech sounds);
- length of attention span and the ability to shift the focus of attention from one stimulus to another or to integrate different channels of attention (e.g. visual and auditory);
- self-esteem;
- motivation;
- satisfactory health.

When considering learners with specific language difficulties, it is usually their verbal memory that is impaired at any or all of the three stages. They will, however, have strengths in other areas, such as visual and or kinaesthetic (movement) memory. When encouraging students to use memory techniques, it is important to help them to be aware of areas of strength, so that weaker areas (e.g. verbal memory) can be supported. Significant improvements can be made when a range of strategies and techniques are employed by both the teacher and the learner. Suggested strategies will now be described using headings to demonstrate which stage of the memory process is being used.

Strategies for the learner

It is important to provide opportunities to discuss and try out a range of strategies in a light-hearted way. This will enable the learner to discover which strategies are going to be of most use. After this, prompting use of strategies prior to a lesson and evaluating their effectiveness afterwards can promote carryover of these strategies. The learner may or may not be aware of the strategies he or she currently employs, or of the relative strengths in his/her memory system, and a process of making these aspects explicit may be necessary. This will demonstrate to the pupil which self-help strategies are already in use and will provide an opportunity to give positive feedback and praise about these aspects.

Acquisition

The learner should be aware of the need to:

- minimise distractions (such as a window view or noise from a corridor), for example, by choosing a different place to sit;
- look at the speaker to maximise the sensory input received;
- admit when they have become distracted and ask for a repetition (it is important that this should be seen as a positive course of action by teaching staff as it is a difficult thing to own up to!);
- ask when a spoken instruction seems too complicated or was delivered too quietly or too quickly.

Retention

The learner should become accustomed to:

- clarifying what they have been asked to do (e.g. 'So you mean I have to ... ');
- verbally rehearsing instructions or information (i.e. saying it over again aloud or in their head). This will enable the student to remember verbal information in order to write it down or will facilitate transfer of information to long-term memory;
- visualising the language they hear (i.e. converting spoken words into pictures in their mind);
- recording key information using symbols (simple drawings that are meaningful to the learner) or words (see Chapter 1);
- asking for time in order to think and make use of the above strategies.

Retrieval

This stage may involve recall of subject specific vocabulary, an event, or sequence of events. Many students with verbal memory impairment experience frequent word-finding difficulties. This is something we all experience to some degree, for example when struggling to recall the name of a film watched only last month. The experience is always accompanied by extreme frustration, as there is a sense that the word is 'in there somewhere' but just cannot be reached. Word-finding difficulties can vary from day to day or during the course of the day depending on a number of different factors. Recent research has highlighted a number of teaching and retrieval strategies that are helpful (see Hyde-Wright *et al.* 1993 and Easton *et al.* 1997). It is important for anyone experiencing word-finding difficulties to develop a range of strategies to reduce frustration and facilitate retrieval, including:

1. thinking about the meaning of a word, including:
   - what category does it belong to? e.g. it is an insect?
   - where do you find it or what do you do with it?
   - think of another word that is similar to it.
2. thinking about the sound structure of the word, including:
   - what is the first sound?
   - how many syllables does the word have, or is it a long or a short word?
   - does it rhyme with anything?

3. use of gesture to show the shape of an object or to show what you do with it.

4. drawing a representation of the word (e.g. an icon – see visual shorthand Practice Paper in Chapter 1).

5. thinking of a sentence with the word in it and leaving a blank (e.g. pins and … needles).

Some learners may also experience difficulties in recalling a sequence of instructions or events, for example remembering the order of a science experiment or of a story. They may start to retell the sequence of events and become muddled or confused. In this case, retrieval can be facilitated by the following:

- remembering how many events or parts of the instruction there were, then counting each one of your fingers;
- visualising the story or experiment (e.g. 'seeing' the events in your head and being aware of the sequence – like rewinding and replaying a videotape in your head);

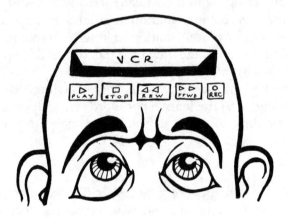

- taking responsibility for using information given by the teacher (for example, information given on the board or in a handout), in order to check the sequence before recalling it.

Strategies for Teachers and Support Staff

Acquisition
Remember to:

1. gain the pupil's attention before an instruction is given (e.g. say name and establish eye contact).

2. sustain attention by using multisensory approaches:
   - visual (pictures, objects, posters, cartoons, keywords/symbols, colour coding, gesture);
   - procedural (movement, role-play, rhythm);
   - smell and taste (where possible!);
   - music.

An excellent resource promoting multisensory approaches to curriculum concept learning is *Language Concepts to Access Learning* (Rinaldi 1998).

3. refocus attention by highlighting the most important information.

4. give clear explanations to the learner so they know what is expected on them (e.g. write an outline of tasks to be covered on the board).

5. Modify information given orally by:
   - avoiding unnecessarily complex sentences and by trying to 'chunk' language into short phrases (e.g. instead of 'Collect the pile of science books that are in the large stock cupboard and hand them out to anyone who needs one', say: 'Go to the large stock cupboard. Collect the science books and hand them out.');
   - repeat important phrases, information and words;
   - try not to speak too quickly;
   - avoid idiomatic language if your aim is to impart an important factual message, as the learner may become distracted by trying to unravel the true meaning behind your words. If you do use an idiom, check the understanding and explain what you really mean (e.g. 'Hold your horses');
   - introduce new words/concepts gradually and check understanding before putting them into a teaching context.

We all tend to remember information when it is presented to us in an outstanding or bizarre way. Try to employ these tactics (where possible!). Motivation is an important factor in sustaining attention to a task. Organise rewarding tasks for the end of the lesson (e.g. a game or quiz) and give occasional reminders about these 'carrots' during the lesson.

Retention

If you want to increase the chances of your learner retaining information, try the following strategies:

1. The 'primacy and recency' effects are well-documented phenomena (i.e. that we tend to remember information taught at the beginning and end of a lesson more easily). This can be capitalised on by introducing short breaks during the teaching time where the pupils do something different (e.g. walking around the room or completing a diagram). In addition, as the middle part of a lesson is vulnerable to memory lapses, include the most exciting or outstanding feature at this point.

2. Revise and recall after each *learning break* (e.g. discussing what was liked/disliked about the topic previously covered, summarising, word definition quizzes).

3. Focus on the key concepts/words being introduced and increase chances of retention by:
   - checking and explaining meaning by relating the word to its category, relating it to words that are familiar and then giving an example in context, for example; 'Frustrated – it's a feeling, a bit like cross, when you can't do something you want to do – I felt frustrated when I couldn't play football because it was raining';
   - organising information given to pupils and maximising visual support. Use word trees and mindmaps to show how words are organised hierarchically and are related to each other;
   - discuss the sound structure of the word; for example, how many syllables does it have? What is the first sound and does it rhyme with anything?

Retrieval

As described under 'learner strategies' word retrieval difficulties can cause embarrassment and extreme frustration. The following techniques are aimed at reducing these feelings in the learner.

- Allow the learner time to make use of their strategies when they are trying to recall a specific word – count to ten in your head before trying to help. (Remember how irritating and distracting it can become if someone suggests a long list of possible names to you when you are trying to recall the title of a film!)
- Encourage the learner to use self-help strategies (see strategies for the learner earlier in this chapter).
- If the pupil is unable to recall a specific word, accept their explanation or description of the word, which will often demonstrate good understanding of underlying concepts.
- If the pupil is really struggling, give forced alternatives to minimise feelings of failure (e.g. is the word *mammal* or *insect*?)
- Use different modes of recall to reduce pressure on spoken recall (e.g. written responses and use of drawing). Word-finding difficulties often become more severe when people are placed on the spot and given a time limit.

As described above, the pupil may find it difficult to recall sequences of events or a series of instructions and may become muddled when trying to do so. Remember to try the following to minimise confusion and muddle:

- Make the sequence of events clear by displaying a numbered step-by-step approach to the task, which the pupil can refer to in order to support recall. This could be written on the board or backed up by symbols.
- Again, encourage the learner to use self-help strategies (see strategies for the learner earlier in this section).

Practice Paper

Reading comprehension and keywording

The most noticeable aspect of understanding what you read is how much easier it is when you know something about the subject or topic that you are reading about. In education this is called background knowledge. Within teaching it has always been assumed that this is the main factor influencing reading comprehension. From a memory perspective we would describe background knowledge as semantic memory. As you read, word meanings and visual images are being activated and developed. Recent research has however, demonstrated that the ubiquitous verbal memory (phonological working memory) is also necessary to the process of comprehending what you are reading. Reading comprehension involves making inferences. Research shows that it is not your semantic memory that is the primary factor in making inferences, but your verbal memory. The key is the ability to actively manipulate the spoken words that correspond to the written words, in your verbal working memory (Oakhill *et al*. 1997, Cain and Oakhill 1997). Pupils with a poor verbal memory often need to reread sentences and paragraphs. They also find it easier to process short sentences.

Despite appearances, pupils who are poor at understanding what they are reading are more likely to be having difficulties in processing the language (verbal memory) than in understanding the ideas themselves (semantic memory). If the verbal memory load is reduced for pupils, then more of them understand what they are reading. Textbooks that avoid long sentences might communicate far more than those that do not.

There is an even more efficient way to engage directly the understanding (semantic memory) of pupils, and that is to identify the keywords in the text. In the earlier discussion (Chapter 1), we noted that the semantic memory is not structured as sentences but as word meanings and images. The semantic memory connects keywords together rapidly and efficiently. As well as underlining keywords in text, they can be removed and rearranged in the form of a diagram. This could take the form of a hierarchy, web or objects and connections (see Chapter 1). More meaning can be included by using icons.

For students with learning difficulties, worksheets and textbooks are increasingly available that make extensive use of keywords and iconic diagrams. This is done in the name of differentiation. It is often reported that pupils sitting next to students using material like this often ask if they can use it rather than the full written texts that they have been given. They find this material easier to understand. It is easier not because it is simpler but because it reduces the overall amount of information. Sadly there is some sort of educational machismo associated with the ability to handle complex verbal information. The ability to remember detail is valued above the ability to understand.

We have conducted a large number of workshops where we help the participating teachers realise that they can comprehend passages from a keyword diagram more easily than from the full written text. This is true even when the comprehension questions have been constructed based only on the full text and ignoring the key word process.

Reading comprehension turns out to be yet one more area where there is a need to restrict and control the influence of verbal memory in the name of more effective learning and understanding.

Descriptive writing

Practice Paper

The strategies described below to develop descriptive writing have been used within specific settings with hearing-impaired students, students with language impairment or those with language processing difficulties. The approaches should be considered for all students experiencing difficulty with verbal memory.

Listening to, recalling and describing a 'story'
Verbal memory is supported by rehearsal, that is, by repeating or saying aloud what you have just heard, such as a phone number or a direction. This can be seen as an opportunity to use the outer voice to support/help the inner voice. Research in this field suggests that

speaking out loud and self-voice have a part to play in reading (Baddeley 1986), and that pupils (including the deaf) are able to perceive and respond positively to the sound of their self-voice even though their speech may appear unintelligible to others (Lane 1990, Wood *et al*, 1986).

In practice it seems that hearing-impaired students and students with verbal memory and processing difficulties benefit from listening to their own recorded voice. Strategies to support verbal working memory are seen as helpful for deaf students to master the steps to develop narrative skills, in order to be able to describe a story and produce narrative in the final written form.

In a local project in 1994, Honor Andersen piloted a scheme in a primary unit involving the development of narrative skills starting from the child's own story/account, in their own language, supported by inner voice:

- The child taped a short personal event in natural language.
- The child drew a picture of the event.
- An adult transcribed the account, using the child's language. This could be written with the picture or put onto a computer. The child listened to their taped voice as they looked at their picture and the written word.

She found that disaffected children became more focused and motivated as they began to experience the connection between speaking, listening and the written language.

Story retelling

A number of strategies involving much repetition and rehearsal are being used to help hearing-impaired students develop narrative skills. They are similar in principle to strategies helpful to hearing children with verbal memory problems. Lewis and Wood are using self-recorded videos to help deaf children with the development of narrative skills. One such strategy using a self-recorded video was described by Lewis (1997).

- The story is read to the student who listens.
- Rehearsal; student recalls what they can of the story – no pictures, no prompts.
- The videoed response is replayed; student re-listens to self-voice.
- Student writes what they have said on the tape (this can be using shared writing or using visual representations of the student's choice initially).

In this first presentation and cycle, Lewis explains how the initial recall of the story may be only a few words. There is likely to be a significant pause as the student waits for an (over) helpful adult to either furnish the answer for the student or to give 'helpful' questions such as 'and the wolf said ... ?' etc. Such prompting is not forthcoming. However, small the amount recalled, this is replayed together and written by or with the student, in order for the written word to be linked with spoken language. In this first cycle, by receiving no visual or verbal prompts, the student begins to understand the task and to work on their language processing and recall.

For the second cycle, the story is reread while the student listens, followed by verbal rehearsal and retelling again. This time the student should recall more as the task is better understood. There is more focus on language processing and less expectation that an adult will jump in with answers (preventing the need to develop one's own skills). The story is reread and the cycle is repeated about four or five times using a shared writing approach.

The spoken narrative develops, which is rewarding each time the student watches themselves on video. The written narrative develops, always matching verbatim the language the student has used.

With this kind of experience/practice it is hoped that hearing-impaired students will better develop skills to be able to recall and retell verbal information, and also to be able to describe in written form something which they have been told. It is a task that hearing-impaired pupils have great difficulty with. This kind of process becomes a prerequisite in Key Stages 2 and 3 and its establishment is generally assumed in the teaching of Key Stage 4.

Story writing

Strategies for developing story writing for hearing children with processing difficulties at Key Stages 1 and 2 are discussed by Jenny Jones in her Practice Paper on supporting verbal memory in Chapter 3. Stories can use visual cues to support the storyline. These can take the form of a sequence of photos to create a story or drawing the story on a sequenced picture sheet. This can then form the basis for writing and later redrafting. Stories can be the child's version of a familiar story with the language rehearsed, the story acted out, key figures in the story drawn and laminated, before words and sentences are created from this multi-memory source. Children can be helped to create a fact/fiction imaginative story around the support of a factual information base or structure. When stories are told by children they can be taped or scribed to recall the storyline for writing. Stories can be created using group writing or shared writing, with children bouncing ideas off each other and taking it in turns to develop the storyline or to write the word or sentence.

Practice: retelling a story and developing a story

Rachel George and Fiona Barton have described the following strategies and resources to help students with verbal memory difficulties at Key Stages 3 and 4.

1. Five-minute and ten-minute thrillers and tapes (LDA). These come complete with comprehension questions and have been used in a variety of ways:
   - they can be used with the comprehension sheets;
   - they can be listened to in order to develop or practise diagramming text, mind maps (see Practice Paper on note-taking later in this chapter);
   - they can be listened to, to retell the story in only ten sentences – to practise picking out keywords. (see Chapter 1 Practice Paper on keywords and icons);
   - the tape of the story can have the questions added to it, for the student to take home and listen to and work on.

The written stories can be used without the tapes and used as a basis to practise diagramming and keywording (see chapter two practice paper reading comprehension) with a view to story retelling.

2. Colour cards (Winslow). Sequencing cards are used to establish a storyline as a basis for verbal exploration. In addition, other stories can be made up using the cards as cues. Cause and effect cards can be used in the same way.

3. Goosebumps cards (Waddingtons). These are used to develop a story theme and to develop recall using visual cues. In this way students can learn to extend memory by using picture images. They involve a sequence of pictures developing a ghost story theme; the sequence and story is extended with an extra image to recall for each additional card.

The above ideas show how students can be given the opportunity within school, to work on developing the skills that they personally need, in order to be able to function within the curriculum. They can have assignments on practising keywording, mind mapping, visual imaging. When they have developed these study skills and also developed greater self-awareness of how they need to work (see Chapter 4) they will be better able to progress in the classroom.

Strategies for processing information: Priming

Memory for, or recall of, information rests upon semantic memory (understanding). A major problem for the hearing-impaired, given their functional language-memory restriction, is to be able to make sense of and understand what they listen to. It is, however, a challenge to many pupils in our schools.

Priming is helpful to us all, but it is frequently overlooked in the classroom. Examples of two different kinds of priming.

1. The familiar example is of being told to listen to a sequence of instructions to be recalled and acted upon, but with clues as to the subject of the activity removed, e.g:
   • The first task is to sort according to colour;
   • The next is to sort according to texture;
   • The programme is consulted with regard to temperature;
   • Commence with the first of the groupings;
     ...and so on.

The critical prime is that the instructions refer to washing clothes in a washing machine.

Someone who has been primed with this information will be able to make better sense of and so recall more than someone without this information (who can probably make no sense of it at all). Visualisation, thinking in images, is impossible without knowing the subject.

2. Priming itself can also be visual. At a signing class, the class was told they would be shown a video of a person telling a story in British Sign Language (BSL), and were asked to recall what they could. Immediately before the narrative, a comic-strip sequence was briefly shown. As a result of the visual priming, it was possible to recognise and to recall some of the signs. Without that visual priming, one of the authors could not have begun the task.

Priming is being 'prepared' before going into a lesson or before listening to a piece of narrative within a lesson. Priming can take several forms:

- being shown the narrative first in a visual form – pictorial /comic-strip/written. (Pictorial or written form should be presented in order or sequence such as left to right or top to bottom to reinforce understanding and recall.)
- being given keywords on topics. As far as possible keywords should be presented in the sequence in which they will occur. This provides a timeline and supports the memory to retain the sequence. It gives a basis for meaning and understanding. Many pupils, particularly the hearing-impaired, need to be cued to attend to keywords.
- having the opportunity to talk about a new topic or story beforehand.

The opportunity to share meaning is important as it enables students to build up their semantic memory (understanding). This is a language process and needs to take into account the child's verbal memory and language level. This will have implications for delivery by providing the need to create opportunities for modified language, e.g. pacing, delivering and pausing to ensure that an instruction or explanation has been understood. In addition, shorter 'chunked ' sentences need to be used where the memory can process the information load at the same time as allowing for natural rhythm and intonation.

There are wider uses of priming in the school setting:

- Where students have been withdrawn for part of a lesson or are returning after an absence, it is difficult to understand what is going on without some form of priming.
- Class teachers may be able to present a visual form of a new topic, or of the completed task aimed for, before beginning instructions or explanations.
- Where keywords or points have been identified in a priming time, support workers can help students to reflect and recall the meaning they reached as they listened in class, by restructuring questions on these keywords or points.

Essay writing

Practice Paper

Students with a history of literacy difficulties are often poor at organising information in essays. At sixth-form college level they can have mastered all the skills of grammar and spelling but still are told that they repeat themselves, fail to include all the relevant points, or go on too long about a particular aspect. We can now see that underlying their original difficulties with literacy was a poor verbal memory. It is this that then creates the later problems with essay writing. The faults that we have just outlined are a result of the poor organisation of information. As we know, this is a key task for verbal memory.

When writing an essay, our semantic memory (understanding) generates many relevant ideas and many that diverge from the topic.

The key ideas, represented by keywords or phrases need to be remembered, placed in a sequence and then recorded. If we have a good verbal memory, this can occur as we write. An idea comes to us and we save it for later in the essay. We also retrieve key facts quickly and easily. Essay writing is, however, so demanding that all pupils and students are strongly advised to organise information in note form prior to writing the essay. For individuals with a poor verbal memory this is an indispensable stage and the whole process has to be followed through carefully. A simple model of essay writing that is adequate for short pieces involves the brainstorming of keywords onto a blank page. If using notes, various keywords can be extracted from them. Once all the essential points have been identified in this way then a sequence or order needs to be established. Numbers can be written alongside each keyword. If ideas travel together they can be given the same number. Another technique is to draw arrows from the first keyword to the next, and so on.

For longer pieces of work, notes need to be used. Notes should be written on only one side of the paper. If two sides have been used then the second side can be photocopied. The notes are then cut up into separate points. This can encompass one or two lines or a whole page. The cut up pieces can then be sorted and resorted until a clear sequence is established. Sometimes they are then stuck on new backing paper. In the memory and ICT Practice Paper in Chapter 1 you can read about how word processing can assist with essay writing.

Practice Paper Note-taking

Like all the topics in this book, we need to cover this area from two points of view. Firstly, from the perspective of the teacher who considers that notes are necessary. Secondly, in terms of the way that the teacher can help the pupil take accurate and accessible notes.

The teacher wants the pupil to have notes that record the information and knowledge that the teacher wants the pupil to know. The highest priority is to ensure that any important details are recorded. In other words, anything that has a high load on verbal memory. The following are examples:

- the planets in order from the sun with their relative size;
- the names of the great classical composers with their country of origin. Other examples of this type would be the names of explorers in Africa or the names of Tudor monarchs;
- laws, equations, formulae or rules to be applied to information;
- types of rock, commercially grown grasses, etc.

These are the highest priority because they are the easiest to forget. Usually it is better to prepare this information for the pupil and to provide it in a handout. Teachers sometimes state that a list of formulae is no good to a pupil if they don't know how to apply them. This is of course true, but a common scenario is for the pupil to recognise an instance where the formula should be applied but not remember accurately the details of the formula.

The next area is that of new vocabulary. It is not enough to simply record the new terms. The pupil needs to record alongside a simple version of the meaning. Often the teacher embeds what is in fact a new term for the pupil in a discourse about a subject. The meaning can be worked out, but is not simply stated. Terms that may be new to some or all of the pupils need to be listed in a dictionary format. The use of icons alongside definitions helps considerably in conveying the meaning (see the keyword and icons Practice Paper in Chapter 1). Again, these can be given out as prepared handouts.

In discourse and by illustration and example, enriched and adapted in conversation with the pupils, teachers try to develop the semantic memory or understanding of their pupils. This description already emphasises the multimedia/multi-memory approach that we have been advocating. In their own note-taking, pupils need to be encouraged to take the same approach. Rarely is it necessary to take notes that are full sentences. This is a burdensome and unnecessary expectation on pupils. Keywords and phrases linked by lines, arrows and personal symbols are the most efficient and accessible way of taking notes. A full diagrammatic approach can be taught and used by pupils. This is sometimes called *mind mapping*. The pupil records the keywords and links them with lines. Although the objects and connections diagram is the most accurate (see the semantic memory section in Chapter 1), it is hard to do in note-taking.

The best approach is to use semantic webs. As the teacher starts on a topic, this is written as a keyword, or phrase, in the middle of the page. Important points made about the topic are written round the side and linked with arrows to the topic. Small sub-webs often develop from one of these words. When the topic shifts, a new central word is written. At the time, or immediately after, new linking lines, (maybe using different colours), extra words written on the lines to describe the nature of the link and little icons can all be added to enrich the semantic record.

Perhaps the most surprising aspect of note-taking is that it is a skill that is not taught to pupils. As with many of the topics covered in this book, those relating to Key Stages 3 and 4 can all be grouped together under the broad heading of study skills. Increasingly, schools are allowing time for this subject and so hopefully these vital skills will begin to be taught.

Chapter 3

Memory and education

Overview

This chapter sharpens the focus on the relationship between children's memories and the demands that education places on them. It therefore examines the main learning tasks (which we call learning goals) that confront children in school. At the primary phase of education, these are the basic skills of oracy, literacy and numeracy. Of relevance at the secondary phase in particular is a consideration of the different demands that different curricular areas make on young people's memories.

As a fundamental psychological construct, memory is surprisingly absent in current educational thinking. This is no doubt linked with the general decline in the influence of academic psychology in education. In recent years, there has been a huge amount of attention devoted to what children must learn at school, and a corresponding neglect of *how* children learn. By contrast, the 1960s witnessed a greater degree of influence from developmental psychology. Since that time, 'psychology' as a knowledge base, discipline and profession has developed enormously, but with some notable exceptions (such as in proposing models of literacy acquisition); this development has largely proceeded apart from educational theory and practice.

One reason for this may be the absence of a general 'theory of learning' that could be applied to the context of school. Although models and information-processing metaphors abound within cognitive science, teachers are not sure what to make of them and how they might be applied to develop a greater understanding of how children learn.

The application of models of memory has been similarly problematic. Learning and memory are difficult to disentangle. Learning has traditionally been distinguished from memory on the grounds that it involves acquiring knowledge and skills, while memory involves retaining them over time. However, such a distinction is difficult to maintain in practice, as the overlap is considerable: learning can be seen as a process of building up networks of associations which are modified in the light of subsequent experiences. Such networks have a clear relationship to 'semantic memory'.

We believe that a greater understanding of how children learn must incorporate contemporary models of memory. The 'multi-store' model of memory, developed in the late 1960s, which distinguished between a short-term and a long-term memory store, was unable to account for our complex and varied representation of the world. The account of human memory that we gave in the opening chapter attempts to do justice to the complexity of our memory processes, and the range of individual differences that exist.

Individuals differ in their preference for dealing with different kinds of information. In a companion volume to the present work, Riding and Rayner (1998) have developed the construct of 'cognitive style' to account for individual preferences in processing information (the holistic–analytic dimension) and in representing information (the verbaliser–imager dimension). Once differences in cognitive style are acknowledged within education, links with teaching methods and approaches will inevitably be made.

The notion of teaching to strengths is well established within the field of special needs teaching, but less so within the mainstream. The influence of theories such as Gardner's multiple intelligences (1983), and their implications with respect to preferred ways of learning, constitutes a strong intellectual background within which the study of individual differences is currently located. Much interesting work is being done in the field of adult learning, where it is appreciated that different methods suit different people and different approaches suit different subject matter.

Another reason for the neglect of memory in school-based education lies in its association in the minds of teachers with rote learning. 'Discovery-led' learning has been the contemporary wisdom within primary education since the Plowden Report, and although it has faced challenges from both inside and outside the educational establishment, it continues to play a considerable role in the thinking of teachers – at least at the level of an espoused theory. Classroom-based research (Alexander 1995), however, calls into question the appropriateness of a 'discovery' mode of teaching in situations where direct instruction would be more economical (in terms of teachers' time), and more efficient (in terms of children's learning).

The kinds of task for which direct instruction is better suited are those where basic associations need to be learnt and remembered by children. The nature of the association is likely to be arbitrary and therefore not amenable to being 'solved' or 'discovered'. Learning letter sounds and names and the numbers 0–9 are examples of this kind of knowledge. As we saw earlier, our verbal memories are engaged with this type of learning. A sizeable proportion of children have difficulties with learning these associations in their first year at school, and ways of improving their learning of and memory for this knowledge are outlined below.

The re-establishment of rote-learning in school is emphatically not our aim, however; rote learning has always placed youngsters with verbal memory weaknesses at a disadvantage. Indeed, we would seriously question the utility of attempting to 'train' this memory, and the bulk of our recommended teaching strategies concentrate on getting round difficulties by using relative strengths and external memories. It is this important aspect that can be overlooked in discussions of curriculum differentiation. Thinking of differentiation in terms of addressing individual differences can be helpful in two respects. First, it prompts teachers to think about their own preferred modes of learning (and therefore of teaching). Secondly, it helps to separate what is to be taught from how to teach it.

As we show in Chapter 2, an exclusively verbal presentation of a task or topic is subject to the bottleneck of the limited-capacity verbal working memory system. The questions that then arise are:

- In what other forms could the information be presented?
- How is the especially salient information presented?
- How can the verbal load and content be simplified?

Similar questions can be asked about how children in turn show their understanding and knowledge:

- In what form is the information required to be presented?
- Could the means of presentation be altered or supplemented?
- Can they identify what works for them?

It would be a mistake to think that curriculum differentiation is only relevant for the 'special needs' child. When we look at effective teaching, we see that it uses a range of methods of presenting information. This makes it more likely that what is experienced (or 'learnt') becomes subsequently available (or 'remembered'). Our everyday experience is that we do not tend to remember what is not interesting or important to us. We remember things that have an emotional impact. We remember things that are unusual or unexpected. We remember better when learning is embedded in a unique context. (One of the authors remembers vividly a Geography field trip that took place 30 years ago, because it involved taking to the air in a light plane. The important point is that facts; verbal and semantic memories learnt on this trip are also well remembered. They were also part of the 'episode'.)

Equally, we do not underrate teaching strategies that pupils rate as being helpful, e.g. (Cooper and MacIntyre 1993) such as recapping on the previous lesson, giving an overview of the prospective lesson and providing learning breaks. These suit all learners, as indeed do a number of other contemporary teaching practices such as pupil self-assessment, peer teaching and peer review. What is common to these approaches is the notion of making knowledge and skills explicit, and in doing so, making them available to consciousness.

Curriculum subjects and memory

No discussion of memory and education would be complete without a consideration of the differing demands that curriculum subjects place on memory. Our relative ability at a subject reflects various factors, but over a long period of time undoubtedly the most dominant factor is how the subject fits over our own memory profiles. Different subjects fit different memory profiles. Foreign language learning places a considerable demand on verbal memory, while physical education emphasises procedural memory. Below, we have identified the profile for each of the standard subjects. In theory, it is possible to assess each child for their cognitive profile, i.e. their strengths and weaknesses in the various memories. This could then be matched with the demands of each subject. It would then be possible to predict which subjects the child will be relatively good at, and which ones they will find relatively difficult. In turn, this could influence how they are taught. The matching of pupil and subject memory profiles could also point to how to teach particular subjects to particular pupils.

English

The key to English is vocabulary. Vocabulary learning is strongly related to verbal memory. Research shows that until the age of six, the ability to retain what is said is the main factor in the size of one's vocabulary (Gathercole *et al.* 1992). After six, the main influence becomes reading. Comprehending what you have read is, throughout, also strongly influenced by verbal memory. Background knowledge is also vital. This is pure semantic memory. Understanding what you are reading is easier and more likely to be remembered when the content is pictureable (the long-term visual component of semantic memory). Nobody remembers the exact words of a novel they have just finished reading, but it is possible to have a detailed memory of narrative and characters, stored as visual images derived from the author's descriptions.

Extended written pieces such as essays require semantic memory (for meaning links) and verbal memory (for finding words, structuring sentences and ordering the sequence of ideas).

Mathematics

Mental mathematics takes place in the verbal working memory. This memory is also required for remembering procedures and equations. The knowledge structure of mathematics is very precise, and seems to be dependent on the exactness of spatial thinking. A mental modelling ability, visualising diagrams and dimensions, is required. Aspects of long-term visual memory are involved. Semantic memory is probably less important than it is for any other academic subject. The skeletal structure of mathematics is the key to its mastery.

Physics

This subject is a marriage between mathematics and semantic memory. The semantics need to be supported by special episodes (practical experiments – where the world can be experienced differently). Treating experiments as an expendable luxury is a big mistake. A simple description of experiments does not have the same strength in episodic memory. Verbal memory is also involved because of the amount of new vocabulary and the amount of arbitrary detail in formulae and equations. At its most theoretical level it demands, like mathematics, considerable spatial thinking.

Chemistry

A similar subject to physics, but with a decrease in the mathematics and an increase in verbal memory (new vocabulary and poorly connected detail such as the periodic table). It also has a larger semantic content.

Biology

Similar to chemistry but with a further increase in semantic content and verbal memory, and a further decrease in mathematics. In so far as it is experimentally based, it shares with the other sciences the embedding of learning experiences in episodic memory.

Design and Technology

A practical subject in terms of any artefact that is produced, therefore at this level it has a strong component of procedural memory. Demonstration and practice are the key to learning/remembering in procedural memory. There has been a reduction in this emphasis in recent years and a bias towards design rather than realisation. Design without practical skills has severe limitations. Semantic memory, primarily visual, features strongly in design. The emphasis on verbal memory is at a minimum and is only involved in instructions, particularly where there is no accompanying illustration or demonstration, and the learning of new vocabulary. The 'words' part of semantic memory does, however, feature in the area of reflecting on the results of practical activity (e.g. evaluation).

Physical Education

A subject dominated by procedural memory and thus dependent on demonstration and practice. There is increasing content in this subject and a corresponding increase in semantic memory demands. Skill building through sports continues to predominate as a separate area however, and 'knowing how' retains its superiority to 'knowing that', by virtue of this.

Music

In studies of human memory, music is something of a mystery. Clearly, some fundamental cognitive processes are involved, but these are found in a scattered way. There appear to be different ways of being 'musical'. It is also a subject that benefits from early experience, continuing throughout development. We suggest that those who are interested consult one of the specialist books on the psychology of music.

History

This is a subject best initially built on episodic memory (story). New topics always benefit from a return to this episodic base. Semantic memory quickly builds from this episodic base, both memories sharing, as they do, the media of language and imagery. Semantic memory comes to dominate this subject. Gradually, however, there is an increasing emphasis on verbal memory, as history contains a considerable amount of detailed information, and not just the obvious one of dates. Pupils are often caught out by this subject. They do well when there is a large emphasis on episodic and semantic memory (GCSE), but struggle when detail becomes vital in constructing and illuminating arguments (A level and above). You need to have a strong verbal memory to handle this subject at an advanced level.

Religious Education

This subject is completely dominated by episodic (story) memory and semantic memory (meaning). Verbal memory is involved, at a relatively low level, in special vocabulary and in the detail of religious observance.

Geography

This is a true multi-memory/multimedia subject. It is the most tolerant of different routes to competence and mastery. Its semantic content contains a very high level of visual material, right up to the most advanced form of the subject. Many geographical concepts are best communicated visually, through maps and plans, such as town plans or an aerial photograph of a river valley. It is possible to identify a developmental sequence in the understanding and interpretation of maps, starting with simple locational plans, bird's eye views and picture maps, through to Ordnance Survey maps, where conventional symbols and other kinds of feature representation replace pictures.

This subject lends itself to a variety of other media, such as film, CD-ROM and the Internet, while field trips and school visits enable pupils to experience the subject matter at first hand. Visual, semantic and episodic memory all feature strongly in this subject, with verbal memory becoming more prominent when written accounts are required.

Languages

Verbal memory dominates the learning of foreign languages. Recent research shows very clearly that how good or bad a child's verbal working memory is predicts how good or bad they will be at foreign language learning (Service 1992). Recent teaching has emphasised the contexts and scripts within which the language is used. This is the natural starting point of learning a native language, i.e. the language used is part of the situation. This approach makes the language more practical, e.g. what to say when you want to get on a bus. Episodic memory is being used in this form of teaching. However, most episodes have their equivalent in English and it is very hard to graft a foreign language in. Actual experience of speaking the language in those situations is required in order to use episodic memory most effectively, which is why foreign exchanges can be so effective. The only way to free the vast burden on verbal memory is to teach the underlying structure of the language, thus developing a child's language awareness (meta-language). In recent times, this has been an unfashionable approach to modern language teaching. Memory and learning studies consistently show that organising information is the key. In teaching bilingual pupils, it is good practice to have opportunities to compare the structure of the two languages. Mastery of the structure of any area of knowledge is therefore fundamental. There are, moreover, sound developmental reasons why the aping of native language learning does not work.

Information Communication Technology

This subject links directly to issues of memory and learning, because the technology involved calls us to re-evaluate the kinds of information we want pupils to know directly (knowledge in the head) and that which we want them to be able to access (knowledge in the world). Within this subject there is also the distinction between learning about computing and learning with a computer. The former requires episodic and semantic memory, while the latter involves greater reliance on visual and procedural memory. By creating external memories and enabling their routine retrievability, computers vastly reduce the demands made on verbal memory and information handling (the working memory aspect of verbal memory). The on-screen organisation of information using windows (frames) and icons uses the organising principles of visual semantic memory, while the integration of written/spoken text with graphics and diagrams define contemporary notions of multimedia representation. In Chapter 1 we have a Practice Paper on this topic.

Overview ## Key learning goals at the early stages

We turn now to the acquisition of the basic skills of reading, writing and maths at the early stages of education. There is growing evidence that future difficulties with basic skills acquisition can be predicted at an early stage. Equally, there is evidence that individual differences in these skills, as measured for example by baseline assessment, are amplified over the years through Matthew Effects – 'the rich get richer, the poor get poorer' effects noted by Stanovich (1986). While educational underachievement is a complex phenomenon with many contributing causes, the identification of children who may be 'at risk' of failure would be one significant step towards raising achievement. We find in our individual casework a consistent association between verbal memory weaknesses and poor progress with literacy. This is confirmed by research (see Chapter 2). Admittedly, correlation does not imply causation. Nevertheless, we would advocate the assessment of verbal memory as an essential part of drawing up a cognitive profile of any child who finds literacy learning difficult. The aim of such a profile is to establish strengths and weaknesses in order to plan suitable learning programmes.

Although we present examples of successful teaching approaches in this section, we do not aim to provide general guidance for the teaching of literacy and numeracy, or even a guide to what is usually referred to as multi-sensory teaching. There are plenty of other books that cover these topics. Instead, we keep a 'memory' perspective uppermost in considering the use of mnemonic approaches. Jenny Barrett and Pam Fleming present a method of teaching letters and letter sounds. Jenny Jones then considers the powerful aid to memory that the child's own voice represents. This theme is developed further by Carol Hodgson in presenting an approach based on singing.

Spelling is then considered, particularly the early stages, where its step-by-step nature is evident. The process by which sounds need to be kept in mind in a sequential manner during spelling is a clear example of phonological memory function. However, the role of the visual sketchpad is also highlighted in the process of 'picturing' words as visual wholes and recalling the visual–spatial arrangements of their individual letters. The existence of pupils who read adequately but who spell badly is strong evidence for specific visual–spatial memory weaknesses. For these pupils, spelling mnemonics can be of valuable assistance. The range and type of spelling mnemonics are then explored.

Early development in mathematics appears to rely on visual–spatial thinking that links to the young child's experiences with objects in his environment. Necessarily associated with this is the learning of the precise uses of words such as 'middle', 'next', 'first', 'after', 'between', etc. Barrett, Daines, Donlan and Fleming have carried out research into this area with four-year-olds (Barrett *et al.* 1996). Learning the notation of mathematics can prove to be difficult for some children once they start school. Numeral recognition and matching numerals with number quantities are the mathematical equivalents of learning letters, and Jenny Barrett and Pam Fleming outline their system for teaching these associations to children with language difficulties.

Reading

Overview

When young children say 'I know that word' (referring to a printed word), they usually mean 'I know what it says' rather than 'I know what it means'. (Both assertions may be true, of course.) This difference in emphasis reflects a debate about the nature and purpose of reading instruction that has been going on for years. An over-emphasis on what words and texts 'say' detracts from what they 'mean', according to one view. This is countered by the argument that readers are simply unable to access the meaning of text unless they can identify the words on the page with a high degree of accuracy. The former position highlights reading comprehension. The latter position highlights word recognition. It is currently accepted that the two aspects are separable.

In Chapter 2, we considered reading comprehension as part of the wider issue of language comprehension. In this section, we consider word recognition from a 'memory' perspective.

At a fundamental level, word recognition must rely on memory. The brain naturally perceives patterns and regularities in recurring visual symbols, and to the extent that these symbols are repeatedly presented on the page, so they will be remembered as letter strings. Children with good visual memories may remember a large quantity of words in this way, and by doing so, come to a basic familiarity with the orthography of English.

Orthographic, or whole word, strategies for reading should not in principle be affected by verbal working memory weaknesses. In practice however, we find that children with poor (phonological) verbal working memories nevertheless frequently have difficulties at the stage at which they are trying to establish a basic sight vocabulary of words for reading. Why should this be so? We think that the same mechanism that leads to slower acquisition of spoken vocabulary (see Chapter 2) may also lead to slower acquisition of a sight vocabulary. It is the impermanence of the sounds of spoken words that makes it hard for pupils to build connections between spoken words and their printed equivalents. This is especially true when the spoken word itself lacks the quality of 'salience' in the child's own vocabulary. Many high frequency, or functional, words lack this quality (e.g. 'and', 'is', 'to', 'for'), as compared with the names of concrete objects ('tree', 'bird', 'school'), actions ('run', 'jump', 'look') or proper names ('Mummy', 'Jason'). These functional words are not memorable in themselves because their meanings (in spoken language) and boundaries (in the speech stream) are not clear. As a result, children cannot easily construct an icon (visual image) for them in their semantic memory. Hence their lack of concreteness makes it hard for these children to build connections between such spoken words and their written orthographic patterns. The result is that the hardest words to learn in the early stages of reading are often the words most frequently encountered in text. In Chapter 1, we looked at how the use of signs can improve this learning for children (Ripley and Daines).

Additionally, when children are taught to decode letters to sounds (phonics teaching), the dual processes of breaking words down into their component letter sounds and blending them back into words make demands on working memory that may prove too great. Where speech sound, i.e. phonological, awareness is poor, the difficulty is compounded. Indeed, clinical experience suggests that weaknesses in these two cognitive processes frequently coincide, so that when assessing phonological awareness, using an instrument such as the Phonological Assessment Battery (Frederickson *et al.* 1997), it is not always possible to separate the relative contributions to the child's difficulties of memory and phonological awareness weaknesses.

The teaching approach that favours splitting up words into onset and rime (c-at) rather than phonemes (c-a-t) can be justified on the grounds that it lightens the memory load as well as on the grounds that it corresponds more closely to the developmental sequence suggested by research (Goswami and Bryant 1990).

However, the same research highlights the difficulties that many young children have in analysing the sounds in words. Pointing out that words are made of letters and that letters have sounds raises the issue of how to identify these sub-units of language. Referring to them by their alphabetic names (ay, bee, cee) is one approach. Referring to them by their sounds (ah, buh, cuh) is another. Both approaches potentially lead to confusion when phonics teaching gets under way. An alternative approach is to give them a character or image as in Letterland (Wendon 1989). In this approach, each letter has an identity, so that 'C' becomes Clever Cat by assuming the image of a cat's face.

To the child, Clever Cat becomes the means by which the letter shape is remembered, and with which the initial sound, or onset, is associated. The image and name aspect of letters, introduced through Letterland, makes early learning of the alphabetic system possible. Furthermore, the narrative brings the characters alive (Clever Cat knows how to cook, cross the road and count to a hundred), setting them firmly in the child's episodic memory.

Letters and letter sounds – a mnemonic approach to teaching and learning
(Invited paper from Jenny Barrett and Pam Fleming)

Practice Paper

Many children have difficulties with learning the names of letters, letter sounds, and linking the sound to the visual representation (the symbol). Similarly, the names of numbers and the mathematical values attached to them can be equally difficult to learn. It is well recognised that the link between the sound and the symbol, or the number and its mathematical value, is arbitrary. It is necessary, therefore, to help each child to forge a connection between the two. This learning task is not easy, so a more innovative approach is needed to make use of some kind of clue, in order to make more accessible the correspondence between the symbol and what it represents.

One of the most helpful techniques is to use a 'bridge' – to bring the two arbitrary items together by reference to some third item, which is, in itself, more familiar. This 'bridge' provides a more organised relationship between the symbols and what they represent.

Historically, this 'bridge' is known as a mnemonic. The usefulness of mnemonic devices has been recognised for many thousands of years. Cicero (in *De oratore*) relates the story of a Greek poet, Simonides, who used a particular mnemonic device to name corpses of those attending a banquet on whom the roof of the hall in which it was being held had collapsed. Simonides had briefly absented himself from the festivities, during which time the tragedy had occurred.

In the context of literacy, all mnemonics involve making the material more meaningful, fitting material to already learnt frameworks, or elaborating it by images or associations. These might be:

- colour coding (visual memory)
- gestures/finger cueing (visual and procedural memory)
- story links (episodic and semantic memory)
- alliteration (verbal memory)
- geometric shapes framing the relevant phonic units (visual memory)
- any combination of the above.

Idiosyncratic symbol systems have been in use for years by teachers, but in 1973, Lyn Wendon developed 'Letterland' for the teaching of phonics to children with reading and spelling difficulties, which aimed to provide a more standard system of symbols. She says of the system, 'The pictogram might best be described as a piece of pictorial language, strategically placed within the abstract shape so that it can simultaneously endorse that shape and symbolise its sound.' The system thus associates letter sound with picture clues based in letter shapes. Each letter of the alphabet becomes a character who lives in the mythical, magical place called Letterland. The system comprises two sets of picture code cards.

Set 1: introduces the Letterland alphabet with further cards whose characters elaborate how letters change their sounds.
Set 2: has some 60 picture code cards which account for all the predictable phonic events in words.

Piaget has pointed out that letters (and this would equally apply to numbers), lack the critical feature of object constancy. By designing body parts into every letter, the system endows them with that missing element.

Two other important teaching principles are covered:

1. Children animating letters effectively teaches them to 'see' the sounds of abstract shapes.
2. New learning grows out of earlier learning. It is not necessary to suppress earlier learning of single letter shapes in order to progress to letter combinations. 'sh' becomes two well-loved Letterland characters: 's' (Sammy Snake) and 'h' (Hairy Hat Man), with a story to explain the sound attached to the symbol.

For children who have no language difficulties, the language of phonics is difficult enough, but children with language difficulties have specific problems with the language of space, time and order, with colloquial language, ambiguous meaning, pronoun reference and deictic or 'empty' words, such as 'it' or 'that'. Lyn Wendon refers to the 'cumbersome language of instruction' that we use, and those empty words that we use, which she terms 'grey words', all of which are devoid of imagery or prior associations in the child's mind.

Stories ascribed to the characters have information about the letter sound encoded in them. For example, 'Bouncy Ben' represents a noisy (voiced) and explosive kind of sound: 'b'. The alliterative nature of the letter sounds with a good rhythm makes them easy to remember and say.

Many children experience difficulties with writing letters. They frequently do not understand the language of space, spatial orientation of letters and letters within words. The kinaesthetic and tactile approach advocated for the teaching of letter shapes, plus the resources by way of rhyme or story to the parts of the letter, rather than directional (cumbersome) language, simplifies and reinforces learning. The characters all walk in one direction along the Letterland road (left–right orientation), they all look in one direction (to the right), and with a few exceptions the stories all explain why this should be, e.g. 'Zig-Zag Zebra' is shy and therefore turns his back. Upper case and lower case letters are related in both story and character, e.g. Hairy Hat Man is so delighted to be in someone's name or in the first word of the sentence, he performs a handstand.

Practical ways of supporting verbal working memory in literacy

(Invited paper from Jenny Jones)

Practice Paper

When helping a child to try and remember abstract, and initially meaningless, spelling or sound patterns, it makes a lot of sense to use a child's own recorded voice. If the child is listening to a story, full of imagery and emotion, then other types of memory come into play, and it can probably be recalled much more readily. But when trying to teach something detached from the child's reality, and basically unappealing, (especially to a child who has experienced minimal success previously), then more imaginative help is needed.

Using the child's recorded voice at least makes a comforting and arresting link between themselves and the alien world of symbols and written words. If a baby at 18 hours old can pick out its own cry, then the significance must be fundamental. Hearing one's own voice becomes a natural extension of the 'talking to ourselves' that we do in our verbal working memory.

If you think in your own voice, then it should be a compelling and obvious medium in which to embed sounds and ideas, that need to be heard and remembered. The lighting up of a child's face when they first hear themselves on tape is confirmation that attention is well and truly focused, with emotional involvement also.

Children who find it hard to know what a teacher is talking about when initial sounds, for example, are being taught, and who continue to remain unenlightened several years/teachers later, need help to find other ways into their consciousness. Often a mass of visual material (worksheets etc.) have been used, sometimes with good speaking and listening backup, but sometimes in fairly meaningless isolation. These children have failed to remember along this path before, so different channels need to be explored.

Visual channels are well used by today's children (literally, on TV!) and on screen generally. Often, auditory skills need to be sharpened, focused and trained so that children can discriminate between similar words and sounds, and remember them.

The systematic introduction of these sounds and patterns via the child's own recorded voice has been proved to be a powerful way of focusing attention on them, giving them some meaning, and triggering recall. Taping provides an inner voice, an auditory rehearsal that hopefully will be replayed at the appropriate time later.

When using teaching techniques which predominantly highlight one channel (i.e. speech sound input), there is always an interaction between other systems which support this (i.e. visual, kinaesthetic, physical). Here, the auditory is supported strongly by the visual – words, pictures – helping to link the two.

The physical mouth and tongue movements, which create the sound, also play a significant role in triggering recall later. A child may wordlessly make the mouth shape ready to say 'w', and eventually the articulation will follow. Again, in saying the word to hear the final sound, as it is formed by the mouth and tongue, a connection seems to link the sound with the muscular movements, so it is physically felt, as well as heard. It is this physical perception, linked to the child's articulation, that seems to trigger recall and awareness of what the sound is.

Taping

Taping, in the early stages of phonological awareness, is used to help the recognition of what is meant by the first sound in a word, or what it begins with. This is an abstract and alien idea to many children, and means nothing at all to them. Others, with no auditory problems, and from a good language environment, appear to acquire these skills effortlessly. Somehow, a system or framework has to be built up into which other new bits of knowledge can be fitted: a child needs a way of analysing words to be able to get to their component parts, and be able to read and write them.

Making a list of words starting with the letter sound that is hard to hear and recognise, with a picture of that (non-abstract) object beside it, is the first step. At the very nearly stage of phonological awareness, just pointing to each word and picture, as the tape is played and paused, is useful in reinforcing the particular initial sound. Attention and listening skills are a vital part of this, as is making the connection again, between the spoken and written word.

Breaking each word into onset and rime is the next step. Once that can become a habitual way of 'breaking down' a word (exposing the vowel within the rime so that it can be identified later), then that system can be applied to any unfamiliar word.

The final step (which wouldn't be needed if the child were able to remember the whole chunk of rime, i.e. -ook) is to say each letter sound. So the list might read:

sun	s-un	s-u-n
sock	s-ock	s-o-c-k
sat	s-at	s-a-t

The practical task of taping needs a good quality tape machine, with a non-audible pause button, as the recording has to be done in small chunks to accommodate verbal working memory problems. Once the most accurate recording that is possible has been achieved, listening to it while tracing a finger along the accompanying text helps to reinforce the link between the spoken and written word or sound. If a child finds it impossible to reproduce a particular sound exactly, then the teacher's voice can be used briefly to model it.

The part that really seems to make the connection between the spoken and written symbol is the simultaneous writing of what the child is hearing through the headphones as they listen to their own voice dictating it. In this way, while all distracting sounds are shut out, the child's own voice can direct their hand to produce letters to match the ones that the familiar voice tells them to write. If this is cursive script, then the kinaesthetic aspect of that movement pattern can also aid recall.

It is important that the tape is paused (initially by the teacher, later by the child), after the spelling of each letter sound or each chunk, and that there is no interruption. The child often repeats aloud what has just been heard (s-u-n) as they write. This is the echo, the inner voice that will hopefully be replayed later, at the perception of the relevant sight or sound. The success of this lies in how often the child can listen to and write this list on subsequent days, following the same procedure – the more often, the more securely the knowledge can be stored in the memory, and accurately recalled later.

In the same way, words containing rimes (-op, -ent, -ock, -ight) can be listed, broken into onset and rime, then individual letter sounds, and recorded. This can be used to back up Phonological Awareness Training (Wilson 1993). Some children find blends of sounds (tr-, pl-, sw-) hard to hear, say or remember. Recording, with lots of rehearsal to get the sound as accurate as possible, helps to strengthen the ability to reproduce and recall the sound later. The technique can be used to break words into syllables, clapping each one, and recording the chunks to be dealt with one by one (i.e. chim-pan-zee).

It has been found to be a very useful aid in helping children with literacy problems for whom English is an additional language – especially in differentiating between similar vowel sounds – 'e' and 'i' for example. Accurate recording is obviously vital here.

Taping can also be used in group work, but there is obviously more potential for distraction amongst those whose attention skills are limited. But useful groupings of rimes, for example cat, sat, hat, can be recorded individually or in pairs on one day, then an accumulated group recording can be used in a Literacy Hour group session (out of the classroom, to maximise learning potential). Each child can write the word that they recorded on a white board as the tape is playing and pausing. Later, the listening and writing can be reinforced by making individual zigzag books of the same words, as the tape is played and paused.

Taping children reading a book in small chunks, can produce an apparently seamless result. It can raise a child's self-esteem and show them what might be possible. If they then read along with their own voice, this can further strengthen the link between the written and the spoken word. It can increase fluency and self-confidence at the same time.

The procedure of taping/listening/writing needs a good quality tape recorder with (silent) pause control, in the classroom and/or at home, so that adequate rehearsal can take place.

Music and Song
Speech sequences can sometimes be more easily recalled by being located in a musical structure especially difficult, abstract sequences like the alphabet, or time sequences – months of the year, days of the week, etc. Children often run through the sequence musically to find the letter/month – they know it's in there somewhere! It can be used to remember a difficult illogical rime such as '-ight', sung to the tune of 'Clementine'. Just humming the tune can trigger recall of the letter string.

Signing
Signing a letter or word is a good visual stimulus to help recall of an awkward, abstract word such as 'what', for example, or an often confused vowel such as 'e'. Cued articulation can help recall of a particularly troublesome sound like 'th', contrasted with 'f' – the

finger movements linked to the mouth ones, enabling the sound to be recognised or said.

Story writing

Children who have problems putting ideas down on paper, or perhaps just having the ideas, need inspiration and support to get going.

- Just talking about whatever subject makes them excited or interested is a good start – ideas and thoughts can be scribed by a more able writer, (see Figure 3.1) or notes taken, or they can be taped, and the tape replayed in short chunks so that the ideas can be captured on paper.

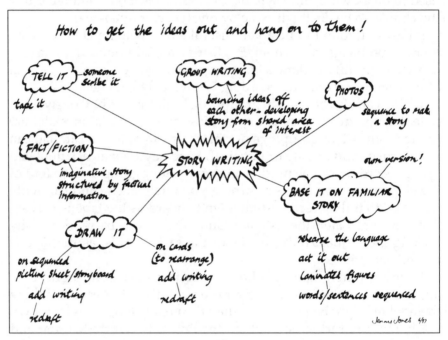

Figure 3.1

- Visual stimulus or memory aid is one of the most useful ways of starting off a piece of writing. Just drawing a picture/making a model of something that is fascinating to the author is often enough to begin the process, and once the first word/sentence is written, the rest is usually easier. Drawings can be sequenced to plan the structure.
- Photos, which can also be sequenced to structure a story plan, are another good starting point. They can also illustrate the finished work.
- Small illustrations within the text are another good way to make writing more palatable for the reluctant writer – a comic-strip format can be good – anything to make the symbolic word more accessible!
- Writing in a group can be a supportive and sometimes inspiring way to write – children taking it in turns to scribe, while everyone else suggests ideas, and the teacher helps to sort and mediate. This models how you can select a good idea from several suggestions, and emphasises the need for rereading, to see how it sounds and to think about what comes next.

- Structuring a story by basing it around non-fiction ideas taken from one or two accessible reference books can help to generate ideas and form a plan of action.
- Flow diagrams, or any visual representation using boxes, arrows, lines or colours – anything that makes the ideas alive on paper and able to be manipulated – can be used.
- Story writing can be supported by basing it on a familiar story, which can be rehearsed and acted out, sequencing words and sentences so that there is a familiar framework to work around and add to.

Singing with Jessica
(Invited paper from Carol Hodgson)

Practice Paper

This idea was used with a child with Down's Syndrome, both in teaching initial letter sounds and a sight vocabulary. It was noticed that this child responded well in music lessons. Her general concentration was better, she listened more intently to instructions, and she enjoyed singing and playing percussion instruments. We therefore decided to try to use both singing and percussion to teach her some initial letter sounds. We began by writing a line of the initial letter sound 'c' on the white board. Jessica had a tambourine, and the teacher a stick to point with. The game was that every time the teacher pointed to a 'c' with her stick, Jessica responded by beating once on the tambourine and singing the letter sound. We played all sorts of variations on this basic game including:

- role reversal – Jessica pointed and I sang and played;
- tempo variations to the pointing;
- pitch variations;
- character variations; monster singing, baby singing;
- loudness;
- different percussion instruments.

We then added one letter at a time and sang lines of different letters. We always worked from left to right across the board. Sometimes I wrote the letters in paper, rather than on the white board, but Jessica preferred the board. Later, as she began to be able to write some of the letters, she wrote the letters for me to sing.

We have also used this method to teach Jessica to read some of the high-frequency sight vocabulary words for reception. We have made up sentences together, using topics of interest to Jessica, and incorporating the target words. So, for example, a recent 'singing story' was:

> Jessica and Sarah went in the car.
> We went to McDonald's.
> We can see McDonald's.
> We like McDonald's.

Initially, Jessica sang this as a whole song as I pointed to the words for her. When she pointed and I sang, she often accidentally left words, or whole sentences, out. I always sang exactly what she pointed to. She found this very funny, and took full advantage of it, but also became far more aware of individual words within a sentence. Singing letters and words has certainly been by far the most successful method of teaching Jessica early reading skills. She appears to be far more motivated, concentrates better, stays on-task for a longer period of time and retains what has been taught more consistently.

Overview   Spelling

Young children's early attempts at spelling offer a window into their emerging understanding of the written code and knowledge of the alphabetic system. At the very earliest stage, there may be superficially little evidence that the child is aware that there is an encoding process involved (translation of a speech code into a written code). Letters and letter strings may be randomly selected to represent words. Letters and numerals may be selected interchangeably, and the left-to-right writing convention may be broken. The first word that is typically learnt is the child's name, which is reproduced as a visual whole in much the same way as a drawing. It is quite possible for a child at this stage to build up a bank of words for writing in a similar fashion.

Memorising the shape of words is an inefficient approach to learning them. Far better to concentrate on letters: if they are to progress beyond a logographic stage to an alphabetic stage (Frith 1985), the child must start learning the links between speech sounds (phonemes) and written symbols (letters).

As an encoding process, spelling consists of writing down 'sounds'. It presupposes a number of sub-skills. First, the ability to isolate individual words from the speech stream. Secondly, the ability to analyse words into phonemes. Thirdly, the ability to apply letter–sound correspondence rules. Even with regularly spelt words, these skills are not necessarily acquired in a straightforward way (with irregular words the difficulty increases further). Much of the difficulty inherent in spelling at the early stage lies at the phonological level. Sounds – whether phonemes or larger units – are not easily detected within words by young children.

The task of linking spoken language to written language is complicated more by characteristics of the former than by the latter. A solid visual familiarity with the 26 letters of the alphabet is a necessary but far from sufficient condition for learning to spell. The real source of difficulty lies in the discrimination, recognition and recall of the 44 phonemes of the English language, i.e. the sounds that the child makes when he speaks. By providing activities that help to foster his ability to hear and remember these sounds, the teacher is providing an essential platform for literacy acquisition.

The strong association between phonological awareness and literacy needs to be acknowledged, but elaborating it further goes beyond the scope of this book. What is noticeable from the observations of young children's early spelling attempts is the role of their own speech in making the task manageable. Speaking the word out aloud, and segments of the word, serves to assist the process of writing the letters. This process, called articulatory rehearsal, is essentially a mapping process whereby sequences of sounds are mapped on to letters. Verbal working memory plays a central part in enabling them to hold in mind these sequences while letter shapes are being recalled from the visual–spatial memory. In the terminology of Baddeley's model, it is the 'phonological loop' that enables phonological information to be maintained and refreshed through rehearsal (which can be vocal or sub-vocal).

In addition to articulatory rehearsal, written spelling also involves a movement component. This is both a potential asset and a disadvantage. To the extent that letter shapes have been mastered, writing words and saying them out aloud simultaneously serves to reinforce memory. To the extent that letter shapes have themselves to be constantly recalled, there are competing demands on memory. Conscious recall requires the involvement of verbal memory. Handwriting, by contrast, is built up over time through repetition and practice to the point where it is embedded in procedural memory. Where a strong process (procedural memory) can be brought in to support a weak process (phonological/verbal memory), a teaching approach that uses the former is likely to be successful.

Getting children to learn spellings by writing them out from memory (look-cover-write-check), as opposed to simply copying them out, is good practice, provided that the words chosen are in their reading vocabulary. An additional stage is recommended for those children who 'lose' phonological information easily: look-say-cover-write-check. By encouraging an association between the word's appearance and its pronunciation, visual and phonological information is combined. Writing the word from memory whilst articulating, in order, its component sounds serves to reinforce the patterning process.

When children get to the stage of recognising and reproducing common spelling patterns, their spelling difficulties are by definition less likely to be phonetically-based, deriving instead from the irregularities of English orthography, multi-syllabic words and confusion about rules (e.g. suffixing rules). It is at this stage that spelling mnemonics can be helpful. These can be classified into at least four types:

1. First letter mnemonics
   - Because: **B**ig **E**lephants **C**an **A**dd **U**p **S**ums **E**asily
   - DOES: **D**addy **O**ften **E**ats **S**weets
   - PEOPLE: **P**eople **E**at **O**ranges **P**eople **L**ike **E**ggs

   The same principle can be applied to 'tricky' letter strings at the end of words.
   - -IGHT: **I** **G**o **H**ome **T**onight
   - -OULD: **O** **U** **L**ovely **D**uck
   - -OUGHT: **O** **U** **G**reat **H**ungry **T**iger

2. The small word within the larger word.
   - PIECE: a **Pie**ce of **Pie**
   - PEACE: the **Pea**s began to fight and then made **Pea**ce
   - FRIEND: keep **End** on the end of Fri**End**

3. Phonological distortions, e.g. to make silent letters speak.
   - WED NES DAY
   - FRU IT: Where's the apple? I fru it (threw it) away.

4. Rhythm and song.

Singing a few lines from the familiar song 'A Windmill in Amsterdam' may help the -ere/-eir/-air/-are spellings:

'Where on the stair
Right there
Little mice with their clogs on
Well I declare
Going clip clippety clop on the stair
Oh Yeah!'

It can be seen that semantic (meaning) and episodic (story/scenes) memories are explicitly being called on in many of the above examples. Spelling mnemonics are most likely to be remembered when they are personalised and made meaningful to the learner as it is the quality of the encoding that makes future retrieval more likely. For the interested reader, *Cued Spelling* (Topping 1988) takes this approach further.

Overview **Mathematics**

Mathematical thought has its origins in the child's encounter with the world of objects. By manipulating objects – sorting and ordering them, matching like with like and assessing their quantity – the young child establishes early mathematical concepts. It is this connection with the physical world that teachers have exploited in making mathematics accessible. The use of physical objects – bricks, cubes, beads, counters etc. – is actively encouraged right up to the intermediate stages of the subject. Seeing the physical representation of quantity – as an array of counters, for example – is the basis for the creation of a corresponding mental image, to which a verbal label, or number name, is attached.

It is commonly assumed in our educational system that counting is the necessary intervening stage. Physical contact with the objects being counted certainly helps with the mapping process that we call one-to-one correspondence, and an ability to recite the number series (rote count) is a prerequisite. However, counting is not the only way into early number ability. It anyway carries with it some potential pitfalls – in the act of counting, young children can easily lose track of the objects they are counting and/or get the number sequence wrong. Additionally, if numerical symbols (numerals) are introduced before they develop the associated concepts of quantity, they can be pitched prematurely into abstract ideas. The early introduction of written notation (i.e. mathematical signs) can serve to compound the difficulty.

Comparisons with other European countries show that written mathematics is introduced relatively early in England and that mental mathematics is encouraged to a lesser degree (the National Numeracy Project is challenging this). The use of apparatus that encourages a visual approach to number patterns and relations seems to facilitate mental mathematics later on, so that children can literally see numbers and number bonds in their mind's eye. The use of such apparatus (e.g. the Slavonic abacus and Catherine Stern's material) raises vital points about human number ability.

We share with many other animals an ability to perceive the number of objects without actually counting them, up to five or six. This perceptual ability is ignored in early number teaching where counting accurately is pressed on children. The ability to accurately verbally count and move forwards and backwards through the spoken sequence, i.e. 98 + 4 understood as 99, 100, 101 and 102; is widely thought to be the basis of numeracy.

Nevertheless, children and adults who have unreliable verbal counting can show excellent knowledge of number value, particularly with money. Research shows that some children with very poor verbal working memories, who are, as a result, unreliable counters, nevertheless have a normal grasp of place value (Doulan and Gourlay 1999). Our knowledge of number value is actually a visual ability. In our mind's eye (sketchpad memory) we literally see the relative distances between numbers. Reaction time experiments have long shown that children find it easier to distinguish numbers that are literally 'further apart' – e.g. 1 and 8 – than those that are 'close together', e.g. 7 and 8.

This visual arrangement is often used by young children to help their number recognition. They can be seen looking into space, at an imaginary number line in their sketchpad memory, as they rehearse the counting sequence from the beginning, to the spoken number that corresponds to the visual number they are trying to recognise. They then say it out loud. Visual number lines are a vital part of early years numeracy teaching, as they support all children's remembering, as well as being essential for some children.

Similarly, the use of Stern's material is being shown to be effective with all children in some local schools known to the authors. Numicon, as the system is called, is a teaching approach and a programme of practical arithmetic that develops mathematical thinking through visual images or icons. The apparatus itself consists of plates that represent numbers 1 to 10 in a range of colours, pegs that build number bonds with the plates, and overlays that act as baseboards. The progression of activities starts with pattern matching. Next, the apparatus is ordered: children are not asked to write numerals until they can order the apparatus and assign number values to it. The next step is to encourage the children to find 'how many' without counting, and to relate the answer to the number line. Numerals become meaningful because of their prior association with visual imagery. Basic addition and subtraction processes can be introduced simultaneously, as relationships (e.g. between 10 = 5 + 5 and 10 - 5 = 5) are grasped visually before they are formally introduced using conventional notation. Numicon can be regarded as a bridge into number in much the same way as Letterland is a bridge into reading. Both share the feature of using children's natural strengths with visual recognition (see Chapter 1) in order to learn what are, in effect, unnatural symbolic systems.

The need to keep track during counting puts pressure on verbal working memory, and it is not surprising that different cultures at different times have devised techniques that get round the difficulty (many of these techniques involve using parts of the body as mnemonics). Mental calculations have the characteristic of requiring some information to be temporarily stored while further processing is carried out. Addition (with carrying) and subtraction (with decomposition) are examples. Oral recitation of times tables is another. Given individual differences in verbal working memory, there will always be individuals who find these difficult. This does not invalidate the argument that the majority of young children could benefit from alternative approaches to the number system at an early stage.

Note: Numicon is available from Numicon Image Learning Systems Ltd., 12b/c Orleton Road, Ludlow Business Park, Ludlow, Shropshire SY8 1XF.

Practice Paper

Remembering basic numbers
(Invited paper from Jenny Barrett and Pam Fleming)

As was stated earlier, the 'bridge' between mathematical symbols and what they represent can present difficulties for some children. In this case, the mnemonic devices most useful are:

- colour coding (visual memory);
- alliteration (verbal memory);
- kinaesthetic and tactile feedback (movement memory);
- visual distance (visual number value).

All these have been combined into a system used primarily with children who have a language disorder characterised by word-finding difficulties. Because of this, i.e. the disorder, they may have acquired other mathematical skills, out of the usual sequence of learning. The system employs Cuisenaire, the child's ability to count by rote and some understanding of 1:1 number correspondence. Cuisenaire rods represent the physical distances between numbers (see the earlier discussion).

Alliteration
Character names of the individual numbers are alliterative in nature, e.g. Timmy Tortoise for '2', Freddy Frog for '4', similar to the type of names used in Letterland, e.g. Bouncy Ben for 'b'. The names also encode further information about mathematical value, such as Freddy Frog has *four feet*, and Sammy Snake has *six stripes*. This reflects the pattern observed in Letterland, where information about the letter sound is encoded in names and stories.

Kinaesthetic and tactile feedback
The character's shape frames the number, providing the possibility of kinaesthetic and tactile feedback, particularly if a range of different texture materials is used.

Colour coding
The system depends upon:

- the child being able to count purely by rote;
- the colour of the Cuisenaire rods and the colour of the character being identified.

For example, when teaching a child the number name of '4', a single white cube representing the value of '1' is placed on each foot of Freddy Frog. These are then counted and matched to the pink '4' Cuisenaire rod. The child then uses verbal recall and, subsequently, rehearsal, saying '4' out loud and tracing the number shape on the pictogram. Over time, the child comes to associate the colour pink with the number '4' and the letter shape, so that the need to count individual cubes becomes unnecessary.

The whole process can be further reinforced by colour crayons used to write the numbers. The characters devised are as follows:

Timmy Tortoise   = 2
'Threepio'   = 3
Freddy Frog   = 4
Silhouette hand
with fingers
and thumb spread = 5 – this is accompanied by a gesture with
                                          fingers spread wide

Sammy Snake   = 6
Sidney Soldier   = 7
Ollie Octopus   = 8
Naughty Nick
(from Letterland)
with a hammer
and nine nails   = 9
Two silhouette
hands with fingers
spread wide   = 10 – this is accompanied by a gesture using
                                            both hands as above.

This system has been specifically devised for children with a particular type of language disorder, i.e. difficulties with word finding which is affecting their ability to recall the names of letters and associated number values.

Comment from the authors

This represents the most intensive mnemonic support we know of for teaching children to recognise and recall the numbers from 1 to 10.

Chapter 4

Meta-memory and personal organisation

Overview　At the end of the overview section on human memory we defined meta-memory as the ability to be aware of your own remembering and forgetting. It is advisable at this point to reread the last few pages of that section. The key points are:

1. We gradually become aware of our memory and slowly learn what words such as 'remember' and 'forget' mean. This process can be clearly seen at about the age of six. By ten years of age, children's awareness is very similar to that of adults. Although, as this book demonstrates, we can constantly improve our knowledge and develop better strategies.

2. The first key stage in meta-memory is learning to rehearse what you have been told, or what you have told yourself. This means that you can deliberately keep information in your working verbal memory. This can be learnt by younger children but is generally observed around seven years of age.

3. By eight or nine, children can be taught to use visual shorthand.

4. By ten years of age children have a well-developed sense that they can 'intend' to remember. They are also aware that they can refresh their memories. See the end of Chapter 1 for a more detailed discussion of this.

5. The use of external memories develops during the teenage years. What can you remember yourself and what do you need to use an external memory for? This takes some sorting out and continues to be mixed up with our reliance on the memories of other people. As we saw from our secondary school survey, pupils still tend to rely on other people to act as external memories for them. Very few teenagers use diaries. They routinely forget birthdays and remember Mother's Day when reminded or when they see the advertising (here, they are remembering by visual recognition rather than by verbal recall). Generally, the first external memories used are the lesson timetable and the homework diary. Primary teachers and parents anticipate the organisational demands of secondary schools and tend to be apprehensive for the children.

They overestimate the difficulties of the lesson timetable and of 'finding your way round a large school', and underestimate the difficulties of the homework diary. Lesson changes are carried out in groups and rapidly become routine movements signalled by bells. Children also use their underestimated visual–spatial memory to rapidly master the geography of the school. Taking the right books and materials to the lessons can be another matter. Some of the most poorly organised pupils take every possible book around with them. Lesson timetables need to be included in homework diaries and used as part of a 'planning and preparation for school' activity that takes place at home. The effective use of a homework diary constitutes a major change in personal organisation for pupils. Despite this, they are very rarely taught how to use it. Raising the children's awareness of their own memory processes should be the context within which the homework diary is introduced.

We have already used the term 'personal organisation', because our ability to organise ourselves is inextricably linked to our ability to remember what we need to do. It is our verbal memory, and to a lesser extent our procedural memory, that carries the information needed. This burden can only be eased with the use of external memories. Pupils with poor verbal memories generally have poor personal organisation. Teachers have long observed that pupils with reading and language difficulties are frequently poorly organised. We now know that the common base is a weak verbal memory. All pupils need awareness-raising in respect to their memories when they begin secondary school, and the topic needs revisiting during their secondary school career. Some pupils have significant problems with personal organisation and they need training and support in using external memories.

In the Practice Papers that follow this brief overview, we consider a number of important aspects of personal organisation. First, we look at supporting younger children in the primary classroom. Secondly, we consider the challenge of mastering the school day. Young children need their activity to be planned for them and they need to 'recognise' what to do rather than 'recall' what to do. They also need to learn clear routines and activity 'rules'. Some children have a good memory for the sequence of events while others need visual reminders. This is true for the majority of four- and five-year-olds. Children as young as this are rarely able to use their verbal memories to store information about sequences of events. Teachers are sometimes frustrated that children have forgotten important changes to routines despite constant telling. They are also surprised that children can keep asking when an event that they are looking forward to will occur. Quite simply, their verbal memories are unable to retain the information, so they keep forgetting. Skilled teachers of young children tend to say things like 'After story time it will be your turn to see the fire engine'. When the children ask again the teacher can be heard to say 'Have we had story time yet?' This serves to give the children an 'episode' – experience – that they can use as a reminder.

The following two Practice Papers look at key areas for secondary age pupils: remembering appointments, arrangements and deadlines, and test and exam revision.

Before progressing onto the Practice Papers, let us consider the topic of raising memory awareness in pupils. The first stage is for pupils to experience teaching, and its associated expectations, that itself shows a clear understanding of memory processes. This appropriate experience will help the pupils draw their own conclusions about what helps and hinders their remembering. In this respect, the teachers' and pupils' knowledge of memory advances together. Secondly, pupils should be taught to rehearse information that is primarily stored in verbal memory. This means that repetition and rehearsal need to be teaching practices, where required. We have considered this already: for young children, days of the week, months of the year, number counting and the sounds of the alphabet letters are obvious examples. Other information suitable for older children is suggested in the section on verbal memory. Thirdly, the direct teaching of mnemonics is a powerful way of raising awareness about memory processes as well as securing the retention of important information. The act of using one memory to support another implicitly recognises that the task is one of memory. It also provides the pupils with strategies they can deliberately use elsewhere in their learning. There are numerous examples of mnemonics in this book, and nearly all can be used with children as young as seven, many with children as young as three (Letterland is commonly used by speech and language therapists). Other ways of raising awareness of memory processes are discussed in the Practice Paper on facilitating memory for language in Chapter 2. In this paper, the value of giving pupils simple memory tasks and then asking them to say how they did them is discussed. Our experience with workshops suggests that this approach helps put adults in touch with their own processes. The object is to make mistakes and also reflect on one's own memory strengths and preferred strategies. Below, we have outlined some simple activities. Each one is followed by some questions that provoke reflection and self-awareness.

1. Put out a sequence of small objects, some of which could be repeated. The sequence is viewed and then covered up. The subject has to duplicate the sequence with their own set of objects. Make sure that the subject has more objects than are needed and more than the required number of any one object.
   • How did you remember?
   • Did you see the line of objects in your mind's eye as you were setting out yours?
   • Did you say the names of the objects to yourself?
   • Did you sing the names of the sequence?
   • Did you make the names of the objects into a little story or mental picture?

2. Give the subject a 'sufficiently difficult' sum to do in their head.
   • Did you hear numbers as you were doing the sum?
   • Did you talk to yourself as you did the sum?
   • Did you see numbers?
   • Did you see a sum?
   • Did you see numbers move?
   • Did you forget any of the numbers as you were doing the sum?
   • Did you use knowledge of number relations?

We have used this exercise a lot in workshops. It is surprising how differently individuals do mental arithmetic. This has more to do with memory profiles than how we have been taught. Only those with weakish verbal memories will use visual imagery. Sums can, however, quickly be made too difficult for most people. A mental arithmetic task also gives the best picture of working memory (see Chapter 1). The central executive part of working memory has to juggle the contents of verbal working memory – talking in your head, and the sketchpad – seeing numbers.

3. Ask the subject to copy a sequence of hand taps where the demonstrators hand also changes its shape, i.e. palm flat to fist to index finger pointing, etc.
   - How did you remember?
   - Did you name the hand positions as you saw them?
   - Did you work out what movements to make as you saw the person doing it?

4. Use nonsense words to make up two different counting sequences to five or more. In one sequence use single syllable nonsense words. In the other sequence use two syllable nonsense words. First teach the single syllable sequence, with three or four repeats, and then ask the subject to repeat it. Now go through the same procedure with the two syllable nonsense words.
   - Did you keep reciting the nonsense words so that you could remember them?
   - Did you turn the nonsense words into images made up from similar known words?
   - Did you sing the nonsense words?
   - Did you remember more easily the single syllable sequence?

5. Play Kim's game. Assemble a number of disparate objects on a tray. The subject looks at them for a while and then the tray is covered with a cloth while the subject attempts to remember the items.
   - How did you remember?
   - Did you keep reciting the names of the objects?
   - Did you remember the position of the objects?

These activities can be used with pupils as young as eleven, to raise their memory awareness. Advice can then be given about helpful strategies.

At secondary level, one of the best ways of raising memory awareness is to use a carefully designed questionnaire. At the end of the human memory overview, we looked at the results of a survey carried out in a secondary school. This produced valuable insights for the teachers and pupils. It is also helpful to share one's strategies and methods with each other. Below we have reproduced the questionnaire and encourage you to use it.

Memory questionnaire

1. Would you say you had a poor/OK/good memory? Why did you choose that answer?

2. What sort of things do you forget? What do other people say you forget?

3. How does this affect you
   – at home?
   – at school?

4. What things do you remember well?

5. Why do you remember these things? Do any of these help you? If so, how?
   – pictures, events, stories, scenes, practice, talking to yourself, routines, writing things down, asking someone else to remind you, anything else.

Acknowledgements to Chris Williams, SEN Secondary Teacher, for her role in developing the questionnaire and for being a full research partner.

Practice Paper

Supporting children with memory difficulties in the primary classroom
(Invited paper from Karen Sandford)

The child with memory difficulties, particularly verbal memory limitations, needs a lot of support to help them survive and thrive in the busy mainstream classroom. Meaningful dialogue between teacher(s) and pupil and family needs to be established so that all parties can meet and work together to identify and to learn to support those memories that are particularly weak. There are many strategies that can be tried using multi-memory approaches. Success will ultimately come when the child is independently aware of a difficulty but can overcome it by using a well-rehearsed strategy. This can be achieved through:

- organisational support
- verbal support
- visual support
- rehearsal
- mnemonic strategies
- emotional support.

Organisational support
Poor organisational skills are very often the hallmark of children with memory difficulties. Forgotten equipment, homework and appointments are key indicators. Often, there is just too much to remember, so realistic and *very specific* targets must be set, e.g. '*Bring* PE kit to school *every Monday* and *leave* it in school until *Friday*.' Also, it is very important for the teacher's expectations to be appropriate. Be prepared to provide equipment, e.g. pens, pencils, and have them available as an acknowledged system for any child to borrow. They are not deliberately forgetting and they probably do not feel good about it. But remember to praise them when they have got the correct equipment. Also, help them to set up an aide-memoire system so that they have a 'checklist' of everyday essentials. This could be a laminated bookmark with illustrations and keywords, computer-generated or self-drawn, that the child makes for themselves, which

is stored in the same place, e.g. small pocket of school bag, and referred to at the same time each day, e.g. before bedtime. If this is helpful, bookmark checklists could also be made for each day of the school week to help remember subject specific items (see Figure 4.1).

Figure 4.1 Bookmark checklist

The teacher needs to plan carefully the layout of the room and resources so the children can learn to rely on permanent physical markers to orientate themselves and access things appropriate to the task. When given a list of instructions, the child may at least then be able to get the squared paper because they have remembered where the drawer labelled 'square paper' is, even if they cannot remember how to do a histogram. A clearly legible timetable and date, displayed daily in the same place, provides an habitual support. Simple everyday tasks such as writing the date should not be an unnecessary burden on the child's memory. Similarly, a wallboard designated as a working resource can significantly reduce unnecessary effort and anxiety for the child. Being able to see that visual prompt of the times table [7 x 8] may make it possible to calculate and hold onto the process of solving that maths problem.

Even within a memory-friendly classroom, the teacher will need to keep reminding the child to use the information displayed until they are habituated.

Verbal support

The classroom is a very verbal environment. So children who have memory difficulties has to work extremely hard in order to acquire, retain and retrieve the information they have received. It is important therefore to reduce the information load through language.

Teacher's need to modify their own language by using short sentences in an easily followed sequence and to keep to the point. They will also be a vital role model for the child's peer group, who will also need to speak clearly and concisely for good social interaction. Repetition using simpler synonyms is helpful, particularly where vocabulary may be distractingly complex. Where possible, teachers need to be talking in a dialogue, so that pupils are engaged in continuous verbal rehearsal. Idioms or colloquialisms are best avoided, unless explained.

Visual support

Visual support is critical: the child with memory difficulties needs training and encouragement in visual note-taking. A useful starting point is for the child to 'draw' in sequence the tasks to be achieved. Keywords and images that are graphic and creative and that can become self-generated are very powerful aids to memory. Teaching the child skills in identifying keywords will help them to become more confident and extend their visual note-taking to making webs and mind-maps while the teacher talks. (See Practice Paper on visual shorthand in Chapter 1). For example, in a science topic on the body, the parts of the digestive system can be remembered by:

- handling a 3D model
- making a body map of a child
- or role playing the journey of a chip

before drawing and writing labels on a worksheet of the outline of a body (see Figure 4.2). For the child's own visual notepad, this can be supported further by numeration and arrows and colour to show order or direction or category.

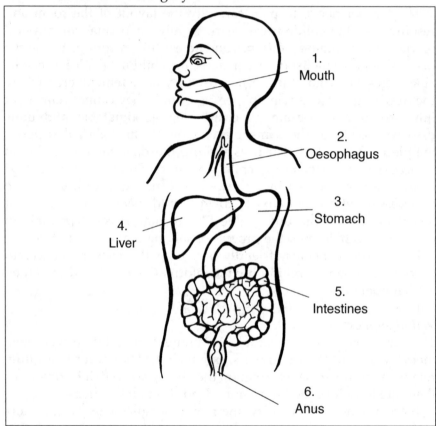

Figure 4.2 Digestive system

Rehearsal and practice

A child's procedural memory can be greatly improved by routines, so daily rituals from the moment they enter school are vital, e.g. lunchbox to dining room, coat on peg, book bag in tray. At first, this may be the only part of the day when the child can do something for himself successfully without verbal thought. Learning by routines is also possible. This works particularly well for tasks such as spelling and tables. A daily routine (a set time and place/resource(s)/procedure) can greatly facilitate procedural memory, e.g. enter class, book bag in tray, get table card and marker card from box, do table card. Add variety to the learning by varying the presentation and the response, e.g. trace over digits on the table while saying aloud, or say aloud times tables but write the answer with a coloured pencil on a 100 table square (so that each table has its own colour-coded pattern). Also, build in a record-keeping system, which the children keep themselves, so that they know that repetition is a deliberate feature of the learning task. A simple reward system, e.g. colouring a square on a grid, will help maintain motivation.

Mnemonic strategies

Mnemonics can be used in a variety of ways and children can be trained in their uses. A lapse in episodic memory can be helped by remembering the context. The child needs to be encouraged to retrace steps so that the forgotten 'item' can be located in context – going back to the changing room may help them to remember where they put their football boots. Similarly, a semantic mnemonic can help link things by word meanings, e.g. for correct hold of the neck of the violin, curve your hand as if cradling an egg.

A movement mnemonic helps memory by linking it to action, so tracing a six-sided shape in the air could help the child to remember a hexagon. Dance routines, particularly where there is music accompaniment in a regular rhythm (e.g. folk dancing) are enjoyable ways of rehearsing memory. Left and right orientation problems can also be helped to be remediated. Mnemonics that help recall by making picture, symbol or positional links can greatly ease the effort of getting things into the long-term memory.

For older children, getting them to visualise their memory as a filing cabinet full of colour-coded curriculum files may help them to remember correspondingly colour-coded keywords for each subject area. There are many examples of spelling mnemonics (see Chapter 3). So much the better if the input can be speech sound as well as visual, e.g. read aloud the letter names and words written on the board: 'u r in for a surprise'. Or maybe add episodic/emotional input too by one child wearing a headband with a UR badge, pretending to surprise another child.

Similarly, there are visual mnemonics to help learn formulae, e.g.

$$S = \frac{D}{T}, \quad D = \frac{S}{T}, \quad S = D \times T$$

All those confusing elements of speed, distance and time can be reliably extrapolated by a strong visual/positional strategy. Similarly, the directional points of a compass can be greatly helped by reading 'WE' for West (East on the horizontal axis. Or *Never Eat Shredded Wheat* will help recall in clockwise rotation all four points of the compass. The author would like to point out that she eats shredded wheat everyday for breakfast, thus showing that mnemonics don't have to be true!

Where the mnemonic has a musicality or rhythm, the strategy is further enhanced, e.g. in the famous case of Henry VIII wives:

> 'divorced, beheaded, died,
> divorced, beheaded, survived'.

It just remains to learn (and remember) the names of the six wives! The sounds of spoken words provide a strong, but sometimes confusing, link. So, picture 'stories' generated, composed and produced by the child to illustrate the words may help them to remember the appropriate word with more accuracy.

Emotional support

Emotion is a big factor in memory. We discuss this in the first chapter. Mental overload generates anxiety and this inhibits good memory function. The teacher is the key player in the emotional life of the child with memory difficulties, and needs to be a constant source of positive support to maintain the child's self-esteem. The teacher can greatly influence learning by maintaining the child's motivation and physiological alertness by, where possible, staging the lesson to a predictable formula.

Ideally the teacher would give:

- a short introduction of 5 to 10 minutes, giving an overview with visual support;
- an example, where possible, of the lesson outcome;
- verbal instructions of the task;
- written and/or drawn instructions on the board in priority order:
  1. must...
  2. should...
  3. could....

Pacing the lesson to include time for:

- learning breaks (e.g. drink of water, song, chat with partner)
- revision and recall
- any homework that needs to be noted

is essential.

Weak memories make all work effortful and the child needs and deserves legitimate breaks. Equally, the teacher needs and deserves the time for a plenary session so that meaningful dialogue that feeds information to remind – 'Tell me what you will read by next lesson?' replaces the often devastating questioning check – 'What have you got to do by next lesson?' Realistic expectations are paramount when working with children with memory difficulties. There are no quick and easy answers. The teaching approaches must be varied so that the child's preferred way of learning is acknowledged. Focusing on their repertoire of strengths will make the learning achievable. The child can then be made aware of when and where aspects of their memory are weak, and learn how to compensate for them. Often, success can be found by the teacher maintaining a positive attitude and continuing to demonstrate belief in themselves and the child. It is all in the rehearsal, and in using two or more of the modalities at a time – visual, verbal, auditory, kinaesthetic – and in a variety of fun tasks and activities.

Practice Paper   ## Mastering the school day

It is well known that the transition from primary to secondary school is a major step. In addition to larger numbers of pupils, regular homework and subject teaching, children must get used to a more complicated organisation of the school day. Secondary schools attach great importance to ensuring that pupils are provided with an accurate and detailed timetable, in recognition of the demands that school places on their personal organisation. A school timetable is an example of an external memory. At the beginning of the school year, all pupils (and especially Year 7) rely heavily on the timetable. After just a few weeks, some will have incorporated it into their routine without making a conscious effort to remember it. Others will still be dependent on it. Using our understanding of memory developed earlier, we can list the different ways in which pupils might remember their timetable without having to refer to it, e.g.:

- 'English always follows maths' (semantic memory – because it concerns a general principle).
- 'This is what I did yesterday/last week/last time' (episodic memory).
- Being on the top floor – Geography is associated with a view of the sea (episodic and visual memory).
- The strategy of following Clement, Jonathan and James who are in the same set (procedural memory).

The children who have the most difficulty remembering the timetable (and personal organisation in general) are those with a poor verbal working memory. It is not simply that they have difficulties with sequences such as days of the week. It seems to be linked with the nature of working memory itself, in that this memory has the wider function of enabling us to forward plan and monitor our plans. In our lives we typically pursue a number of objectives at once. Our ability to set up objectives, to integrate various objectives together, and to keep to them despite competing demands and distractions is the essence of planning. How would a sense of time be related to these functions? Bronowski (1976) suggests that it is the ability to keep several events in mind in the correct temporal sequence that may itself give rise to the psychological sense of time. If this were the case, then time perception would be directly dependent on working memory. A poor sense of time is a typical characteristic of young people who find it difficult to master the school day.

Marking time by means of a timetable is the most common strategy used to overcome organisational complexity in schools. Although primary schools are less complex in this respect, there is a trend in this phase of education towards independent learning and setting children various tasks to organise for themselves. This puts their planning and organising abilities under pressure. For some, the language of time itself may be poorly understood, e.g. vocabulary such as first, second, next, last, before, after, beginning and end. For others, it may be the number and length of instructions that organisational complexity gives rise to. Alexander (1995) is critical of some modes of classroom organisation and pupil grouping that engender an unnecessarily complicated language of instruction on the teacher's part.

Getting a feeling of intervals of time and what it might be possible to undertake in those intervals is an important part of the development of personal organisation. When adults take courses in this area, it is called 'time management'. The existence of such courses suggests that this skill is not easily acquired, even among high-achievers. In schools, the ability to 'tell the time' is often confused with this skill. It is even possible to be good at working out formal problems involving journey durations by train or by air, without having a feeling for time oneself.

An approach that addresses the difficulties that a poor sense of time causes is to present visually a sequence of activities in a symbolic timetable or day plan. This then acts as a physical reminder to be consulted as necessary. This would be the primary school equivalent of the secondary school timetable. More strategically, the day plan can be used as a resource to teach concepts of time directly, such as before/after/next, morning/afternoon, and the days of the week (colour coding the days has been found to be particularly effective).

Where children have severe difficulties in this area, further use of the day plan can be made, through using other memories. For example, the teacher can make reference to it at the beginning of the day, elaborating in further detail the proposed activities. This becomes an event to which episodic memory can be tied: 'Remember what we said earlier'. A visualisation strategy can equally be followed: 'Look at what we are going to do' (cover symbols), 'See a picture of the day plan in your head – say it in your head' (uncover symbols), 'Check to see if it is remembered correctly'.

As a means of reinforcing the sequence, the children can be told to cross out or cover up the activity symbol that has just been completed, before moving on to the next. To encourage them to give an appropriate amount of time to an activity, it is recommended that an egg-timer or clock be used alongside the day plan (see Figure 4.3).

Figure 4.3 Day plan

Practice Paper   **Remembering appointments, arrangements and deadlines**

In Chapter 1, we saw that emotion and intention are important to these memories. All these arrangements are stored in verbal memory. Like other things in this memory, they need to be rehearsed if they are to be remembered. The better you are at this memory, the less you will need to rehearse, or go over in your mind, the details. If your are worried, excited, angry or sad about the arrangements you have made then you will keep thinking about them, and in the process rehearse the detail of the arrangement itself. If an emotion button has not been pressed and you 'couldn't care less' about the arrangement, then you are unlikely to bring it to mind and thus will not reinforce the memory; In consequence, you may well forget it. Strictly speaking, it has been forgotten not because you had no cause to remember it, but because you had no cause to rehearse it. Teachers often activate this process in their pupils by making them anxious about an arrangement, usually by emphasising the consequences of missing it. As long as this isn't overdone, it is an essential strategy within secondary education. Children with very poor verbal memories will need more active support. All pupils would benefit from more reminding than is often offered in the school process.

Our lives are so complex that most of our arrangements and appointments are better and more reliably committed to external memories of one sort or another. Within schools, this takes two basic forms. One is the home–school diary or the homework diary. The other is the use of 'letters home'. Motivation, intention, and the use of routine procedural memory are required if these methods are to be effective. Teachers need to ensure that, through routine, entries are made appropriately in the diary. Pupils need to be taught how to identify and record key information. The hardest thing is to ensure that pupils consult this external memory. They should be encouraged to adopt a routine. Parents could be involved in establishing these. A useful point to insert 'consulting the diary' into the evening routine is immediately after the evening meal. Another point is as soon as the pupil returns home from school, although this can interfere with a needed break from school. Letters and notes home have a high 'loss' rate because they are quite simply forgotten. They are remembered where the pupil has an emotional interest in their content. The only reliable place to put letters is in the homework diary. Teachers could make a point of telling their pupils to do this.

Memory and test and exam revision

Practice Paper

The key to human memory is the accurate identification of the memory, or memories, that you require, and the ability to access them when you need them. How do you know what memories (learning) are needed? We tend to assume that learning and study are valuable in themselves and that, in a general sense, an examination probes what is known. This is a naïve assumption. Assessing an individual's skills and knowledge is a complex process that leads to a great deal of dispute throughout education. The easiest thing to do is to place the pupil on their own and ask them questions. Because this is time-consuming, the questions are asked in writing and the pupils respond in writing. The clearest thing about this process is that whatever else it is, it is definitely a test of literacy. This is explicitly recognised nowadays and various concessions are made for pupils with severe literacy problems. Literacy abilities vary considerably throughout the pupil population, and this will always be true, on an individual differences basis, even when the general standard of literacy is raised. The research into memory also tells us something else about this method. This form of examination also uses the pupil's verbal memory as the intermediary. Whatever the pupil knows has to be put into words.

In Chapter 1, we explored the serious limitations of this memory. Let's rehearse some of them. It is a memory based on the sounds of words. If you are good at it, you can link new word sounds to the objects, people and situations around you; i.e. you can quickly remember names, labels, terms and foreign language words. You can also remember language itself, so you can learn and recite poems, lists, equations and descriptive sentences. You can also organise very effectively all the words and phrases you remember when asked to write your response.

Material in the long-term part of this memory is very hard to hang onto and has to be used regularly. If you are good at this memory you remember a lot of the language which has been used in teaching you and that you have encountered in books. Not surprisingly, when revising for this form of examination pupils try and keep as much as they can immediately available in their verbal memory. They rehearse, usually by rereading, right up to the day of the exam. There is so much that could be examined in most examinations of this type that all pupils are dependent on luck as to which questions are actually asked. How recently they went over the material needed is a key factor in their success. Given the high loss rate of the type of information being examined, and its vulnerability to cramming, the point, purpose and effect of this form of testing needs to be constantly questioned.

Talking and writing don't necessarily reveal understanding. We know that the semantic memory is not organised in terms of sentences. The verbal memory is the main vehicle for expressing meaning. A diagram is another equally valid way of responding to a question about knowledge. Why aren't diagrams accepted as answers to exam questions unless they are specifically asked for?

Written examinations pose difficulties in establishing what a pupil understands. They run into even more difficulties when used to assess an individual's practical knowledge. Again, we have looked at this already. If you have taught somebody how to wean a baby, mend a car, make an object from wood, use a plane of the correct type properly, research tour operators for the best deal, plant bulbs of different types, or any one of a whole host of useful practical skills, you want to know if they can do it, not write about it. If you use this form of exam then the pupils could just read and reread about the practical details and reproduce this in the exam. They may incidentally learn points that they can apply in practice, if, that is, they think verbally about what they are doing when doing it. Written exams on practical knowledge make very little sense.

What does this tell us about how pupils should approach test and exam revision? Much of the emphasis must go on being clear about what form the exam takes, what the questions will be about, what form the questions will be in and what the examiner is expecting as a good answer. As cramming practices attest, the best way to prepare for any test or exam is to endlessly respond to questions of the type that appear on the paper and to have your responses marked by somebody who knows what the marking criteria are. You then need to store as much as possible in your verbal memory. If all pupils are not given equal preparation of this type, then written tests become a lottery, not only in terms of literacy, but also in terms of verbal memory.

When setting pupils revision topics, it is necessary to point as exactly as possible to the memories required. This is best done by setting up the revision topic in terms of a list of possible exam questions. The more organised the information is, the better it is remembered. This should not only influence teaching but also revision. Present the revision topic in a structured way, particularly showing the links between the key ideas. Again, this can be done more effectively through diagramming the links between keywords. Pupils need to be encouraged to work over the information they have. Writing and summarising existing notes on index cards is a common strategy. The act of writing the card helps the mental organisation of the information even if the card is not used again. Word processing and printing out is a similar strategy. Pupils should be encouraged to keyword and diagram their own text. Coloured pens and highlighters can be used on existing notes to link keywords together or to emphasise them.

Finally, be clear to identify the boundaries of the knowledge to be examined. What is the comprehensive list of topics and what is the depth limit of each topic? Secondary school pupils with memory difficulties are helped in practical ways by raising their awareness, both about the use of revision and also about their own learning needs or style. As a result, they can take an active role in planning a revision programme best suited to them.

A local secondary school began the awareness raising by showing such students a short piece from a fast-moving action film with a visual storyline where voices and words were not required (in this instance Arnold Schwarzenegger chasing a suspect). Having followed this short extract avidly, the students were presented, without forewarning, with a worksheet about what had happened, to see if they would have made a good witness. Questions required them to describe specific details: 'There was one witness in the bathroom, describe him'. 'How many were in the lift ?', and so on.

Although all the students had paid attention and followed and understood the short extract they had seen, they found it difficult to answer the worksheet questions. In this assignment the difficulty was either in not being able to convert from the visual detail to the verbal narrative, or not recalling the relevant visual detail. It was not about recalling the verbal narrative, as there was none. Through discussion, the students were able to identify that they would have found it helpful if they had had the questions before they saw the film. They needed to know what was going to be required of them, so that they could better prepare for the task by using verbal reflection during and after the film, and/or by better attending to relevant visual detail.

Having experienced the reality of this, the students were in a better position to see both the need to know the syllabus (to identify the boundaries of the knowledge to be examined, the topics and the depth limit of each topic) and the types of questions which would be asked before the test or exam.

As well as becoming more aware of the need to know what would be required of them, the students were also helped to gain awareness over their personal learning styles.

Each student had a brief questionnaire to help them look at how they learn. Below we have reproduced the questions. The pupils had to put a tick or cross next to each statement:

Section 1 Timing

a. I find it easy getting up in the morning, once my alarm has gone off.
   I have or had a morning paper round.
   I pack my bag for school in the morning.
   I hardly ever miss the bus to school.
   I concentrate better in lessons before lunch.

b. I concentrate better in lessons after lunch.
   I am very busy at lunchtime (seeing friends, playing football, going to clubs).
   I have or had an afternoon paper round/job.
   When I get in from school I usually go straight out again before dinner (to friends, to sports clubs etc.).
   I get on with my homework as soon as I get in from school.

c. I concentrate best later in the evening and do most of my homework then.
   I usually go out after dinner.
   I pack my bag for school the night before.
   I have my main meal at lunchtime.
   I don't watch much TV.

Section 2 Style

a, I can only concentrate on one thing at a time.
   I need to finish something I start.
   I like working on my own in a fairly quiet place with few distractions.
   Once I learn something, I usually remember it.
   I have a good memory.

b. I can concentrate on more than one thing at a time.
   I get bored easily.
   I like to check that I am doing things the right way.
   I find it hard to remember things.

Section 3 Learning

a. I remember pictures better than words.
   I can draw quite well.
   I like using lots of colours on my work.
   I am good at remembering faces or things I have seen.
   I am not a brilliant reader.
   I have a good imagination.

b. I am a good reader.
   I remember things I have heard or read.
   I am not good at drawing.
   I remember words better than pictures.
   I have neat handwriting.

From this, the students were better able to identify the best time in the day when they would be able to concentrate on their revision, what conditions would best suit them when they needed to remember and concentrate, and their kind of memory style, that is, whether they learnt best with pictures and drawings or with words and listening. In this practical way, students with severe verbal working memory problems were helped, through awareness raising, to plan their revision, taking account of their own personal and cognitive needs.

Acknowledgements to Rachel George, Secondary Special Facility Teacher, and Fiona Barton, Secondary SEN Coordinator.

References

Alexander, R. (1995) *Versions of Primary Education*. London: Routledge.

Baddeley, A. (1986) *Working Memory*. Oxford: Oxford University Press.

Baddeley, A. (1997) *Human Memory*. Hove: Psychology Press.

Bahrick, H. P., Bahrick, P. O., Wittlinger, R. P. (1975) 'Fifty years of memory for names and faces: A cross-sectional approach', *Journal of Experimental Psychology*, **104**, General, 54–75.

Barrett, J. *et al.* (1996) The Wallands Project. Unpublished Study, Brighton and Hove LEA.

Bishop, D. V. M., North T., Donlan, C. (1996) 'Nonword repetition as a behavioural marker for inherited language impairment: evidence from a twin study', *Journal of Child Psychology and Psychiatry* **37**, 391–404.

Bishop, D. V. M. (1992) 'The underlying nature of specific language impairment', *Journal of Child Psychology and Psychiatry* **33**, 1–64.

Bristow, J. (1999) Unpublished study of verbal working memory, language and literacy processing in hearing-impaired students. Brighton and Hove LEA.

Bronowski, J. (1976) *The Ascent of Man*. London: BBC.

Brown, A. L., Campione, J. (1972) 'Recognition memory for perceptually similar pictures in pre-school children', *Journal of Experimental Psychology* **95**.

Cain, K. and Oakhill, J. (1997) *Phonological processing and reading comprehension failure: the nature of the relationship*. BPS Research Abstracts.

Conway, M. A. *et al.* (1997) 'Changes in memory awareness during learning: The acquisition of knowledge by psychology undergraduates', *Journal of Experimental Psychology*: **126** General, 393–413.

Cooper, P. and MacIntyre, D. 1993. Perceptions of classroom learning. *British Journal of Educational Psychology* **63**, 381-399

Crystal, D. (1986) *Listen to Your Child*. London: Penguin Books.

Donlan, C., Gourlay, S. (1999) *Knowledge of Numerical Place Value in Children With Specific Language Impairments*. AFASIC Third International Symposium.

Easton, C., Sheach, S., Easton, S. (1997) 'Teaching vocabulary to children with word finding difficulties using a combined semantic and phonological approach: an efficacy study', *Child language Therapy and Teaching* **13**, 125–41.

Eich, E. (1995) 'Searching for mood dependent memory', *Psychological Science* **6**.

Flavell, J. H., Beach, D. R., Chinsky, J. M. (1966) 'Spontaneous verbal rehearsal in a memory task as a function of age', *Child Development* **37**, 283–99.

Frederickson, N., Frith, U., Reason, R. (1997) *Phonological Assessment Battery*. NFER Nelson.

Frith, U. (1985) 'Beneath the surface of developmental dyslexia', in Patterson, K., Coltheart, M., Marshall, J. (eds) *Surface Dyslexia*. London: Lawrence Erlbaum Associates.

Gardner, H. (1983) *Frames of Mind*. New York: Basic Books.

Goswami, U. and Bryant, P. (1990) *Phonological Skills and Learning to Read*. Hove: Lawrence Erlbaum Associates.

Gathercole, S., Willis, C., Emslie, H., Baddeley, A. (1992) 'Phonological memory and vocabulary development during the early school years', *Developmental Psychology*, **28**, 887–98.

Gathercole, S. E., Adams, A. M. (1993) 'Phonological Working Memory in very young children', *Developmental Psychology* **29**, 770–78.

Gathercole, S. E. *et al.* (1994) 'Do young children rehearse? An individual, differences analysis', *Memory and Cognition* **22**, 201–207

Gathercole, S. E. (1990) 'Spearman Medal Address – Working Memory and Language Development: How close is the link?', *The Psychologist* **2**.

Gathercole, S. and Baddeley, A. (1993) *Working Memory and Language*. Hove: Laurence Erlbaum Associates.

Gathercole, S. (1998) *The Structure and Functioning of Phonological Short-term Memory*. Paper for 2nd International ACFOS Conference.

Hintzman, D. L., Caulton, D. A., Levitin, D. J. (1998) 'Retrieval dynamics in recognition and list discrimination – further evidence of separate processes of familiarity and recall', *Memory and Cognition* **26**(3), 449–62.

Hughes, T. (1997) *By Heart: 101 Poems to Remember*. London: Faber & Faber.

Hyde-Wright, S. *et al.* (1993) 'What's in a name? Comparative therapy for word-finding difficulties using semantic and phonological approaches', *Child language Teaching and Therapy* **9**, 214–29.

Idzibowski, C. and Baddeley, A. D. (1983) 'Fear and dangerous environments', in G. R. J. Hockey (ed.) *Stress and fatigue in human performance*, 123–144. Chichester: Wiley.

Kail, R. (1979) *The Development of Memory in Children*. San Francisco: Freeman.

Kennedy, B. A. and Miller D. J. (1976) 'Persistent use of verbal rehearsal as a function of information about its value', *Child Development* **47**, 566–69.

Lane, C. (1981) 'ARROW', in *Ways and Means 3. Hearing Impairment*. Somerset Education Authority. Basingstoke: Globe Education.

Lane, C. (1990) 'ARROW: Alleviating children's reading and spelling difficulties', in Pumfrey, P. and and Eliot, C. (eds) *Children's difficulties in reading spelling and writing*. London: Falmer Press.

Lewis, S. (1997) Presentation to educational psychologists. University College, London, June 1997.

Maccoby, E. E. and Jacklin, C. N. (1974) *The Psychology of Sex Differences*. Stanford, California: Stanford University Press.

Mackworth, N. H. and Bruner, J. S. (1970) 'How adults and children search and recognise pictures', *Human Development* **13**, 149–77.

Marschark, M. (1993) *Psychological Development of Deaf Children*. New York: Oxford University Press.

Marschark, M. (1998) *Interactions of Cognitive Processes and Reading in Deaf Learners: Understanding Differences*. Paper for 2nd International ACFOS Conference.

Meacham, J. A. and Kushner, S. (1980) 'Anxiety, prospective remembering and performance of planned actions', *Journal of General Psychology* **103**, 203–209.

Mitchell, J. (1994) *Enhancing the teaching of memory using memory bricks*. London: CALSC (Computer program based on this by the same author (1998) *Mastering memory*. Communication and Learning Skills Centre: Sutton.)

Oakhill, J., Cain K., Barnes, M. (1997) *Comprehension Skill, Inference Making Ability and Their Relation to Knowledge*. BPS Research Abstracts. *Also* Cain, K. and Oakhill, J. (1997) *Phonological Processing and Reading Comprehension Failure: The Nature of the Relationship*. BPS Research Abstracts.

Paris, S. G. and Mahoney, G. J. (1974) 'Cognitive integration in children's memory for sentences and pictures', *Child Development* **45**, 633–42.

Pickering, S. J., Gathercole, S. E., Peaker, S. M. (1998) 'Verbal and visuospatial short-term memory in children. Evidence for common and distinct mechanisms', *Memory and Cognition* **26**(6), 1117–30.

Rinaldi, W. (1998) *Language concepts to access learning*. Wendy Rinaldi: Surrey.

Ripley and Daines. B. (1990) Unpublished paper on reading and signing. Brighton and Hove Educational Psychology Service, Kings House, Hove.

Riding, R. and Rayner, S. (1998) *Cognitive Styles and Learning Strategies*. London: David Fulton Publishers.

Rubin, D. C. and Rahhal, T. A. (1988) 'Things learned in early adulthood are remembered best', *Memory and Cognition* **26**(1), 3–19.

Semel, E., Wilig, E., Secord, W. (1987) *CELF(R) Clinical Evaluation of Language Fundamentals – Revised*. The Psychological Corporation Jovanovich Inc. USA: Harcourt Brace.

Service, E. (1992) 'Phonology, working memory and foreign language learning', *Quarterly Journal of Experimental Psychology* **45**A: 21–50.

Stanovich, K. (1986) 'Matthew effects in reading', *Reading Research Quarterly* **21**: 306–406.

Stevenson, H. W., Parker, T., Wilkinson, A. (1975) *Ratings and measures of memory processes in young children*. Unpublished manuscript, University of Michigan.

Topping, K. (1988) Cued Spelling Training Pack, Kirklees Paired Reading Project, Kirklees LEA.

Wilson, J. (1993) *PAT (Phonological Awareness Training). A new approach to phonics. Level 1*. Educational Psychology Publishing, University College London.

Wilson, J. (1994) *PAT (Phonological Awareness Training) A new approach to phonics'. Level 2*. Educational Psychology Publishing, University College London.

Wendon, L. (1989) 'Talking about Language with five to seven year olds', in Evans, R. (ed.) *Special Educational Needs: Policy and Practice*. Oxford: Blackwell.

Wood, D., Wood, H., Griffiths, A., Howarth, I. (1986) *Teaching and Talking With Deaf Children*. Chichester: Wiley.

Index

ARROW 36
acquisition 50, 51, 52–3
alliteration 82
anxiety 17, 18–19, 95
appointments, arrangements and deadlines, remembering 94–5

background knowledge 54, 65
basic skills acquisition 68–83
Biology 66
bookmark checklist 88–89, 89
brain-sex differences 1

checklist, bookmark 88–89, 89
Chemistry 66
chunks/chunking 37, 44, 46, 53, 59, 74, 75
classes and categories 7
classroom, memory-friendly 89
cognitive profile 65, 68
cognitive style 63
colour cards 58
colour coding 82–3, 91
computers 7, 13, 30, 32, 33–4, 68
counting 80, 81
Cuisenaire rods 82
curriculum subjects 65–8
cycling 22

day plan 94, 94
declarative memory 3–9 see also episodic memory; semantic memory
descriptive writing 55–59 see also narrative skills, developing
Design and Technology 66
development, studies of 19–20
developmental psychology 62 see also development, studies of
diagrams 7, 7–8, 10, 13, 28, 29, 55, 61, 77, 96, 97
dictation 39
differentiation 28–9, 32, 63–4
digestive system 90, 90
direct instruction 63
'discovery-led' learning 63
doing, learning by 22
Down's Syndrome 78
driving 22

early stages 68–83
education and memory
    curriculum subjects 62–4
    learning basic skills 68–83
    overview 62–4

emotional support 88, 92
emotions 6, 17, 94-5 see also emotional support
encoding see acquisition
English 65
episodic memory
    account of 3–6
    and curriculum subjects 65, 66, 67, 68
    and emotion 6, 17
    and imaginary episode 14
    lapse in 91
    and learning in unique context 4–5, 6, 64
    and learning letters/letter sounds 70
    and procedural memory 10
    and verbal memory 14–15
    brief mentions 21, 22, 80, 93, 94
essay writing 16, 59–60, 65
examinations
    and anxiety 17
    and external reasons for remembering 17–18
    revision for 95–8
    and verbal memory 16, 96
external memories 13, 17, 18, 34, 68, 84, 85, 93, 95
external reasons for remembering 17–18

females 1, 20, 40
foreign languages 65, 67–8
formulae, learning 91
functional words 70

Geography 67
Goosebumps cards 58
grammar 367, 40

hearing-impaired children 35, 36, 39, 43–49, 55, 56, 57, 58
History 66–7
homework 39, 43
    diary 84, 85, 95

ICT see Information Communication Technology
icons
    and computers 33, 34
    and keywords 13, 27, 29, 30–32, 61
    value as memory aid 13
    visual shorthand 24–8
    brief mentions 52, 55, 70
imaginary episode, constructing 14

implicit knowledge 3
individual differences 1, 20, 21, 35, 63, 64, 68
information
    presentation of 64
    strategies for processing 58–59
Information Communication Technology (ICT) 16, 32, 33–45, 68
inner speech 36
input see acquisition
intention 17–19

keywords
    colour-coded 91
    and diagrams 7, 7–8, 13, 29, 61, 97
    and differentiation 28–9
    and essay writing 60
    and ICT 33–4
    and icons 13, 27, 29, 30–32, 61
    and note-taking 61
    and priming 59
    and reading comprehension 54–5
    and retention 53
Kims's game 87
kinaesthetic feedback 22, 82

language 8, 12, 14, 19, 22, 32, 89, 96
    development 36–7
    and memory 35–61
    processing 37
language-impaired children 10, 32, 35, 36, 39–43, 55
languages, foreign 65, 67–8
learning goals at early stages 68–69
lesson timetable see timetable
Letterland 70, 71–2
letters/letter sounds 69, 70, 71–2, 78
letters home 95
lists 8, 13–14, 15
literacy
    and cognitive profile 68
    development 37–8, 48
    and examinations 95
    processing 38
    supporting verbal working memory in 73–7
    see also letters/letter sounds; reading; spelling; words; writing

long-term memory
    semantic 36
    verbal 15, 96
    visual 12, 65

males 1
Mathematics 65, 69, 80–2 see also mental arithmetic; numbers
meaning 6 see also semantic memory
memory awareness see meta-memory
memory difficulties, supporting children with 88–92
memory process, stages of 50
memory span 35
memory strategies see strategies
mental arithmetic 16, 20, 65, 80, 81–2, 86–7
meta-memory 20
    and personal organisation 84–98
mind mapping 8, 13, 28, 61
mnemonics
    account of 5
    direct teaching of 86
    and episodic memory 6, 14
    and numbers 82–3
    and procedural memory 10–11
    and semantic memory 8–9
    and spelling 79–80
    and support for children with memory difficulties 88, 91–2
    teaching letters and letter sounds 71–2
    and verbal memory 16–17
    and visual/spatial memory 13–14
    visual shorthand as 26
models of memory 62–3
movement
    and learning physical skills 22, 23, 24
    memory 22, 23, 24, 33, 47, 50, 82 see also procedural memory
    mnemonic 10–11, 91
    and sounds 73–4
multi-memory approach 1, 21–2, 24, 36, 46, 47, 49, 61, 67, 88
'multi-store' model of memory 62–3

multimedia approach 1, 7, 21–2, 49, 61, 67
multiple intelligences 63
multisensory approach 1, 52
Music 66, 75 *see also* singing

narrative skills, developing 44, 46, 56 *see also* descriptive writing
network *see* semantic web
note-taking 28, 60–1
numbers 11, 69, 71, 80, 81, 82–3, 86
Numicon 81, 82

objects and connections 7, 7
onset and rime 70, 74, 75
organisation, personal 84–98
organisational support 88–89
orthographic (whole word) strategies 70
output *see* retrieval

PAT (Phonological Awareness Training) 38, 75
PhAB (Phonological Assessment Battery) 38, 70
personal organisation 84–98
personal teaching tutor 43
phonics teaching 70, 71–2
Phonological Assessment Battery (PhAB) 38, 70
phonological awareness 37, 38, 48, 70, 74, 78
Phonological Awareness Training (PAT) 38, 75
phonological confusion 37
phonological loop 35, 79
phonological memory *see* verbal memory
Physical Education 65, 66 *see also* sport skills
physical skills 22–4 *see also* practical skills
Physics 65–6
practice 9, 11, 16, 90–1
'primacy and recency' effects 53
practical skills 9, 10, 96 *see also* physical skills
primary level 21, 62, 84, 85, 88–92, 93, 94 *see also* early stages
priming 18, 58
procedural memory
account of 9–11
and curriculum subjects 65, 66, 68
and learning physical skills 22, 23
and routines 11, 90
brief mentions 16, 41, 47, 71, 79, 85, 93, 95
see also movement memory
processing
information 58–59
language 37
psychology 62

questionnaires 2, 4, 87–8, 97–8

re-learning movement skills 24

reading
and analysing sound 70–1
and comprehension 44, 54–5, 65, 69
and phonological awareness 37, 38, 70
value of self-voice in developing 36
and verbal memory 38, 65, 70
and w⋯ recognition 69–70
recall 3, 1⋯ ⋯ ⋯ 48, 50, 51, 54, 56, 57
recognition 3, 18, 33
rehearsal
and descriptive writing 55, 56, 57
and examinations 96
and hearing-impaired student 46
and information to be learnt by heart 16
and meta-memory 84
and remembering appointments, arrangements and deadlines 94, 95
and retention 51
and spelling 78–79
and support for children with memory difficulties 90–1
teaching 86
and verbal working memory 35, 36
and young children 19–20, 35
Religious Education 67
repetition 9, 46, 56
retention 50, 51, 53
retrieval 50, 51–2, 54 *see also* recall
revision 95–8
rimes 70, 74, 75
rote learning 63
routines 90, 95

school day, mastering 92–4
secondary level 32, 43, 44, 45, 46, 47, 48, 62, 84, 85, 87, 92–4, 95, 97
self-voice 36, 38, 46, 56, 73–5
semantic hierarchy 7
semantic memory
account of 6–9
and curriculum subjects 65, 66, 67, 68
and emotion 17
and mnemonics 8–9, 80, 91
and priming 58, 59
and reading comprehension 554, 55
types of connection 7
and verbal memory 8, 14–15, 16–17, 35–6, 37
and visual images 6, 7–8, 19, 28, 29, 30, 35, 61
and words/keywords 6, 28, 29, 30, 35
brief mentions 3, 4, 5, 13, 21, 22, 27, 38, 46, 62, 64, 70, 71, 93, 96
semantic web 7, 61
sentences, difficulty in

understanding 40
sequence 8, 9, 52, 54, 86, 87
sex differences 1
short-term memory *see* working memory
signs/signing 10–11, 75–6
singing 75, 77–8, 80
sketchpad 12, 42, 69, 81, 87
sounds
and literacy 37, 73, 74, 75
and spelling 78
teaching through singing 77
verbal memory based on 15, 96
see also phonics teaching
spatial memory *see* visual/spatial memory
spatial thinking 65, 66
special needs teaching 32
spelling 8, 33, 69, 78–80, 91
sport skills 23 *see also* Physical Education
stories 5, 45, 46, 55–8, 76–7
story boards 28
strategies
for hearing-impaired students 46, 47
and individual differences 1
and intention 18
facilitating memory for language through 49–54
for processing information 58–59
and young children 19
see also mnemonics; name of strategy
subjects, curriculum 65–8
support for children with memory difficulties 88–92

tactile feedback 82
taping 36, 38, 73, 74–5
teaching to strengths 63
tests *see* examinations
time, sense of 93–4
timetable 84, 85, 93, 94
typing 24, 33

understanding 30 *see also* semantic memory

verbal memory
account of 14–17
and curriculum subjects 65, 66, 67, 68, 69
and development studies 19
dominance in educational process 16, 20
and examinations 96
female bias towards 1
and language 35, 36, 37, 38, 39, 40, 41, 42, 43, 44, 45, 46, 47, 48, 49, 50, 51, 54, 55, 56, 57, 59, 60
and learning physical skills 23
and literacy education 68, 70, 73–7, 78–79
long-term 15, 96
and personal organisation 85, 93, 94

and rehearsal 35, 86, 94
and semantic memory 8, 14–15, 16–17, 35–6, 37
working (short-term) 12, 15, 35, 36, 37, 38, 39, 40, 41, 43, 44, 45, 46, 47, 48, 49, 54, 56, 65, 67, 70, 73–7, 78–79, 81, 84, 87, 93
brief mentions 21, 22, 32, 63, 64, 71, 81, 82, 84, 88
verbal support 88, 89
videos, self-recorded 56
visual approach
to learning physical skills 23
to numbers 80–1, 82–3
visual cues/stimulus for story writing 57, 58, 76
visual shorthand/note-taking 24–8, 89–90
visual support 88, 89–90
visual/spatial memory
account of 11–14
and curriculum subjects 65, 67, 68
and development studies 19, 20
long-term 12
male bias towards 1
and mnemonics 13–14, 91
and number values 81
short term (working) 12
sketchpad 12, 42, 69, 81
and spelling 69, 79
and use of icons 32, 33
brief mentions 16, 21, 24, 50, 71, 82, 85, 93
see also visual shorthand/note-taking
visualisation 24, 51, 52, 94
vocabulary 36, 61, 656, 70 *see also* words

walking, re-learning 24
word processing 33–4, 60
word-finding difficulties 51, 54
words
analysing sounds in 70–1
recognition 69–70
and semantic memory 6, 28
and singing 77
and taping 74–5
and verbal memory 36, 39–40, 96
see also keywords; vocabulary; word-finding difficulties
working memory (short-term memory), 12, 15, 87, 93
verbal 12, 15, 35, 36, 37, 38, 39, 40, 41, 43, 44, 45, 46, 47, 48, 49, 54, 56, 65, 67, 70, 73–7, 78–79, 81, 84, 87, 93
writing
learning to write 23, 72
skills 38–39
and spelling 79
and tape-recording 74
see also descriptive writing; narrative skills, developing